The Best of

ALBANIAN COOKING

FAVORITE FAMILY RECIPES

Hippocrene is NUMBER ONE in
International Cookbooks

Africa and Oceania
Best of Regional African Cooking
Egyptian Cooking
Good Food from Australia
Traditional South African
  Cookery

Asia and Near East
Best of Goan Cooking
Best of Kashmiri Cooking
The Joy of Chinese Cooking
The Art of South Indian
  Cooking
The Art of Persian Cooking
The Art of Israeli Cooking
The Art of Turkish Cooking

Mediterranean
Best of Greek Cuisine
Taste of Malta
A Spanish Family Cookbook

Western Europe
Art of Dutch Cooking
Best of Austrian Cuisine
A Belgian Cookbook
Celtic Cookbook
English Royal Cookbook
The Swiss Cookbook
Traditional Recipes from Old
  England
The Art of Irish Cooking
Traditional Food from Scotland
Traditional Food from Wales

Scandinavia
Best of Scandinavian Cooking
The Best of Finnish Cooking
The Best of Smorgasbord
  Cooking
Good Food from Sweden

Central Europe
Best of Albanian Cooking
All Along the Danube
Bavarian Cooking
Traditional Bulgarian Cooking
The Best of Czech Cooking
The Art of Hungarian Cooking
Lithuanian Cooking
Polish Heritage Cookery
The Best of Polish Cooking
Old Warsaw Cookbook
Old Polish Traditions
Taste of Romania

Eastern Europe
The Cuisine of Armenia
The Best of Russian Cooking
The Best of Ukrainian Cuisine

Americas
Cooking the Caribbean Way
Mayan Cooking
The Honey Cookbook
The Art of Brazilian Cookery
The Art of South American
  Cookery

The Best of

ALBANIAN COOKING

FAVORITE FAMILY RECIPES

by
Klementina & R. John Hysa

HIPPOCRENE BOOKS, INC.
New York

Copyright©1998 Hippocrene Books, Inc.

All rights reserved.

For information, address:
HIPPOCRENE BOOKS, INC.
171 Madison Avenue
New York, NY 10016

Cataloging-in-Publication Data available from the Library of Congress

ISBN 0-7818-0609-7

Printed in the United States of America

CONTENTS

INTRODUCTION

Albanians are rightfully proud of their food: delicious and wholesome. All foreign visitors to Albania that we happened to host, as well as all our friends in such different countries as the neighboring Greece or remote Canada, where we have been living for certain periods, have really enjoyed the delicious Albanian dishes my wife served them. They couldn't resist asking her to write down some of the recipes for them or urging her to open a restaurant that couldn't but be a 'smashing success.' It was with this in mind that we decided to choose some typical Albanian recipes from her arsenal of recipes and write this Albanian Cookbook in English.

This book is not meant for those who are satisfied with fast food or canned food, or for those who would readily give up the pleasure of enjoying delicious daily food in exchange of some free time for themselves. It is meant for people who still care for the pleasure of eating good food and are not overcome by the stress of these modern times. It is our firm belief that there are still a lot of such people, who will find it worthwhile to read this book and try the recipes it contains, if not daily, at least on certain occasions, just to have a good time with their families or their friends around the table.

R. J. Hysa

APPETIZERS
MÉZÉ-S:
HOT AND COLD MÉZÉ-S, SALADS

Albanians have always attached special importance to appetizers, probably due to their century-old tradition of welcoming all guests or visitors with real hospitality as soon as they enter their house. Whatever the time of day, the visitor is immediately served a cup of *rak'i*, the national cocktail—a distillate of fermented grapes and a very good appetizer; that, along with a series of appetizers or cold dishes, called *mézé*, prepare the guest for the main hot dishes coming later on. The first cup of *raki* is normally followed by a series of cups through a preliminary meal that may go on for a couple of hours before the host orders the main dishes to be served. Thus, it is sort of a matter of honor for Albanians to always have some nice spicy *mézé-s* at home at any time, as guests may appear without any or at short notice. Friends and relatives are invited to the house, but it is also common for them to drop in without a formal invitation. The guests, who may even be complete strangers to the lady of the house, may not intend or be invited to stay for dinner; nevertheless, they should honour the host's hospitality by enjoying their *rak'i* and *mézé-s* while chatting, laughing and talking politics or social affairs. Some guests may not prefer to drink *rak'i*, which is generally a stronger alcoholic drink than whisky; in such a case they are offered other milder liquors like wine, cherry brandy, vermouth among others, or simply lemonade and juice, served with all kinds of nuts, fruits and other delicacies.

There are hot and cold *mézé-s*. Hot mézés are *fërgesa* (mixture of fried foods), *'kordhëza* or *kukurec* (spitroasted mutton or lamb guts), *shishqebab* (cut pieces kabab), grilled kidneys and liver, beefsteak, meatballs and so on. Cold *mézés* are various salads, *liptao* (cheese salad), sardines, seafood, and pickles.

Most hot and cold *mézés* can be prepared in a short time if not in advance, which is better, as it gives the host or the hostess the opportunity to enjoy the party as much as the guests. The reader will find the recipes for some of the most delicious Albanian *mézés* in the following pages. Unless otherwise mentioned, the recipes will serve 4 persons.

Temperatures are given in degrees (°) Fahrenheit. Those readers who are not familiar with the Fahrenheit scale can consult the following table containing the Celsius equivalents of some temperatures in °F that are most frequently recommended in our recipes:

300°F	=	150°C
350°F	=	170°C
380°F	=	195°C
400°F	=	205°C
32°F	=	0°C (freezing point)
212°F	=	100°C (boiling point)

HOT MÉZÉ-S
MEZET E NXEHTA

FRIED FOOD
FËRGESAT

Fried Liver
Fërgesë me mëlçi

1 pound lamb, mutton or veal liver
1/4 cup oil
1 tablespoon flour
1/2 cup salted cottage cheese
3 to 4 garlic cloves, finely grated
Chili powder
Ground red pepper
Black pepper
Salt

    Dice liver, fry in oil for 5 minutes and remove the pieces from the frying pan. Reserve oil. Add the flour to the remaining oil and sauté until yellowish. Stir in cottage cheese, garlic cloves, chili powder, ground red pepper, black pepper, and salt. Add fried liver pieces and 1/4 cup water or broth, and place the mixture in a baking pan, preferably in an earthenware baking pan. Bake for half an hour at 350°F.
    Serve hot with bread and herbs or salad.
    Serves 4.

Peppers and Tomatoes
Fërgesë me speca e domate

12 green bell peppers
1/2 cup oil
1 pound tomatoes
1/2 cup salted cottage cheese
2 eggs
4 to 5 garlic cloves, finely grated
2 tablespoons chopped parsley
Salt
Chili powder
1 tablespoon flour
1 tablespoon butter

Remove stalks and seeds from peppers, wash, drain, fry in oil, and put them aside. Reserve oil. Peel and dice tomatoes, and sauté them until a thick mixture is obtained. Stir in cottage cheese, stirring continuously for five minutes, then remove the frying pan from heat and add eggs, garlic, chopped parsley, salt, and chili powder to taste. Sauté flour in butter and stir it in. Serve hot in shallow dishes surrounded with fried peppers.

You can also cook this dish by baking the mixture in the oven. In such a case the peppers are diced and fried. Then sauté flour and tomatoes separately, mix them together with cottage cheese and keep on cooking over low heat (about 300°F) for five minutes. Stop heating and add eggs, the fried peppers, hot pepper, grated garlic, 1/2 cup water or broth, and put the whole mixture in a baking pan. Bake for 10 minutes at 380°F.
Serve hot.
4 servings.

Cornmeal
Fërgesë me miell misri

1 cup cornmeal
1/4 cup margarine
3 cups bouillon
3/4 cup salted cottage cheese
Chili powder
1 tablespoon finely grated garlic
2 tablespoons melted butter
2 tablespoons chopped parsley

Sauté cornmeal in margarine over low heat until it turns yellow. Add bouillon, cottage cheese and chili powder, and bring to a boil stirring constantly. Add garlic and cook for 5 minutes. Remove from heat, pour in shallow dishes and sprinkle with butter. Serve hot, garnished with chopped parsley.
4 servings.

OMELETTES
OMËLETA

Tomato Omelette
Omëletë me domate

1 pound tomatoes
4 tablespoons oil or butter
Salt
Pepper
2 tablespoons chopped parsley
4 eggs
2 tablespoons milk

Submerge tomatoes in boiling water for a few seconds so that they can easily be peeled. Remove tomatoes from water, and peel and dice them. Sauté in 2 tablespoons oil for 15 minutes, then add salt, pepper, and parsley. Beat the eggs, adding a little salt and milk and fry them in the remaining oil in another frying pan in a flat sheet (omelette-style). Pour the fried tomatoes in the middle of the omelette and roll into a cylinder. Cut in four serving pieces and serve hot.

4 servings.

Cheese Omelette
Omëletë me djathë

6 eggs
1/4 pound feta cheese
6 tablespoons milk
Salt
Pepper
4 tablespoons butter

Beat eggs, adding cheese, milk, salt, and pepper. Fry the mixture in a large frying pan with the butter. When fried, roll the omelette into a cylinder and cut in four serving pieces. Serve immediately.

4 servings.

Spitroasted Lamb Entrails
Kukurec

Lamb entrails, guts included
Salt
Pepper
1/4 teaspoon oregano
1 onion, sliced
1/4 cup oil
1/4 cup butter
Juice of 1 lemon

Wash the guts thoroughly inside and out. Wash the other entrails as well and leave them in a colander to dry. Then put the guts in a bowl, season with some of the salt, pepper, and oregano, and pour a small quantity of oil on top. Cut liver, heart, lungs, kidneys etc in small pieces and season them with remaining salt, pepper, and oregano. Pierce a long and thin spit through the pieces of entrails, alternating liver, heart, lungs and kidney and placing a thin slice of onion between each three or four pieces. Stick one end of the small intestine to the point of the spit and roll the whole gut around the pieces so that it covers them thoroughly. Put everything into the large intestine and tie its ends using a short piece of the small intestine so that everything stays in place during the broiling.

Mix oil, butter and lemon juice and use this mixture to sprinkle the entrails now and then while broiling them over blazing charcoal, turning slowly but constantly. Keep turning until well broiled and browned on all sides.

You can also bake the *kukurec* in the oven, at 350°F. It is served hot, cut in as many pieces as you choose, and accompanied by salads and pickles.

4 servings.

Shishkabab
Shishqebab

1 1/2 pounds boneless lamb, mutton, veal or pork*
1/4 cup olive oil
2 tablespoons vinegar
1 teaspoon oregano
2 bay leaves
3 small onions, sliced
Salt
Pepper

Cut meat in small pieces (about 1 inch). Combine the meat pieces in a bowl with the oil, vinegar, oregano, bay leaves and thin slices of onion, and let marinate in the refrigerator for 3 hours.

Pierce short skewers (6 inches long) through pieces of meat, placing a thin slice of onion between every two pieces and broil over blazing charcoal, turning constantly until well broiled. Sprinkle with juice from the bowl, salt, pepper, and oregano.

Serve hot, accompanied with french fries and various salads. 4 servings.

*It is recommended to choose boneless meat, leg or round, and clear it of membranes, tendons etc. You can also prepare the shishqebab with mutton, veal or pork, using the same method.

Bowl Kabab
Tasqebab

3/4 cup grated onion
1/4 cup oil
1 pound boneless lamb (or mutton, or pork), cut in chunks
1 cup red wine
1 large tomato, diced
Salt
Pepper
Oregano
1 bay leaf

Sauté onion in oil for 5 minutes in a saucepan. Add meat and sauté until onion is lightly browned. Add wine and put the lid on. After a few minutes, stir in tomato, salt, pepper, oregano, the bay leaf, and 1/2 cup water. Simmer for 1 hour.

4 servings.

Baked Liver
Mëlçi të furrës

You can prepare this *mézé* with veal, beef, mutton or pork liver, with or without bacon.

1 pound liver
1/4 pound bacon, or 1/2 cup oil
1 teaspoon flour
Salt
Pepper

Wash liver thoroughly and put it in an earthenware bowl. Add hot water until half of it is covered, then cover the top half with bacon or oil. Bake in the oven at 350°F for about half an hour, sprinkling alternately with a mixture of flour, salt and pepper and the drippings. Remove liver and stew into a relatively thick sauce. Cut liver in slices and serve in dishes, covering the slices with the sauce.

You can accompany this dish with mashed boiled potatoes mixed with a bit of butter and chopped parsley.

Beef Kidneys with Mushrooms or Artichokes
Veshkë kau me këpurdha ose angjinare

1 1/2 pounds beef kidneys
1 pound mushrooms or artichokes
5 tablespoons butter
1 tablespoon flour
1 cup red wine
Salt
Pepper
2 tablespoons chopped parsley

Cut kidneys in half; take off membranes, excessive grease and tendons, and wash thoroughly. Put in boiling water for 5–10 minutes in order to remove the strong odor. Drain well, dry with a napkin, and cut in slices.

When using artichokes, first remove stems and the coarse bottom leaves, then immerse them in salted boiling water for 10 minutes before frying. After frying the mushrooms or the artichokes in butter, remove them and fry kidney slices in the remaining grease. Add flour, keep stirring until well browned, then pour the wine. Add salt and pepper, fried mushrooms or artichokes and boil everything in a saucepan for about 15 minutes. Serve hot, sprinkling with chopped parsley, accom-panied with French fries.

4 servings

Oven Beefsteak
Biftek i furrës

1 1/2 pounds boned beef
3 tablespoons flour
Salt
Pepper
1/2 cup oil
4 large onions, cut into ring slices
2 large green peppers, grated
6 garlic cloves, grated
1 cup red wine
2 large tomatoes, peeled and diced
2 bay leaves

Cut meat into steaks and beat thoroughly to tenderize. Immerse steaks in a mixture of flour, salt and pepper and put them in hot oil in a frying pan for a few minutes so that a crust is formed. Remove steaks and put them in a shallow casserole; fry onion ring slices in the remaining oil until brownish. Add

grated green peppers and garlic cloves, and keep frying until everything becomes brownish. Add wine, tomatoes and bay leaves, and boil the mixture until a sauce is formed. Pour half of the sauce in the casserole, put steaks on top and cover them with the other half of the sauce. Bake in the oven for about 20 minutes at 380°F.
Serve hot, accompanied with mashed potatoes or French fries.
4 servings.

Stuffed Beef Spleen
Veshkë kau e mbushur

1 beef spleen
1 onion, finely grated
1/2 cup oil
4 tablespoons rice
2 teaspoons tomato sauce
1 tablespoon chopped parsley
3 to 4 garlic cloves
3 tablespoons grated cheese
Salt
Pepper
Oregano

Wash spleen thoroughly and let drain. Pierce through with a long knife to create a pocket inside it. Sauté onion in hot oil until well browned and add rice, tomato sauce, parsley, garlic cloves, grated cheese, salt, pepper and 1/4 cup water and let the mixture simmer until all water is absorbed by rice. Stuff spleen with this mixture, sew it with thread, add oil and oregano and put in a baking dish. Bake at 380°F for 45 minutes. Serve hot, in its own juice, accompanied with salad.
4 servings.

Rolled Ground Beef
Rolé me mish të grirë lope

1/4 pound white bread
1 pound ground beef
1 onion, finely grated
3 tablespoons chopped parsley
2 tablespoons flour
Salt
Pepper
1/4 cup oil
2 eggs, boiled and cut into halves

Dip bread in a little water, squeeze slightly, and combine in a bowl together with ground beef, onion, parsley, flour, salt and pepper. Mix everything into a uniform mass and put it on the edge of some oilpaper (which has been brushed with oil in advance). Shape the mixture into a roll and cut a lengthwise groove into it with a spoon. Fill the groove with the halves of the boiled eggs. Wrap everything with the oilpaper and tie it around with a string.

Put the roll in a saucepan, sprinkle with the remaining oil and bake for about 45 minutes at 350°F. Remove the roll from the saucepan and cut it in four serving pieces. To make sauce: Stir one tablespoon flour in the remaining juice and sauté until brownish. Add 1/2 cup water, season with salt and pepper and boil for 10 minutes.

Serve the rolled ground beef portions in small dishes with sauce.

4 servings.

Spitroasted Lamb
Qingj i pjekur në hell

1 lamb (for roasting)
Salt
Pepper
1 cup lemon juice

Clean and wash the lamb thoroughly inside and out. Remove all entrails, in order to make room for the spit to pass through colon, larynx and mouth. Use a string to attach the backbone to the spit, then season thoroughly with salt and pepper inside. Back legs are also attached to the spit. Rub the outside with lemon juice, season with salt and pepper. Make a strong fire with wood or charcoal over a 3-feet long, 1-foot wide and six inches deep hole dug in the ground and place an X-shaped support for the spit at each of the two shorter sides of the hole. When the fire has burnt down into glowing charcoal, place the spit over the supports and start turning it slowly, sprinkling the meat with a mixture of lemon juice and oil now and then. Turn until meat is tender, increasing the speed with the time. The meat is well broiled when it starts to crack. Serve hot, with salad, fresh onions and garlic, cheese and rak'i, wine or beer.

You can also spitroast a piglet by following the same procedure. Before attaching piglet to the spit, put it in boiling water for a few seconds, then rub the skin to remove all remaining hair.

COLD MÉZÉ-S, SALADS
MEZET E FTOHTA, SALLATAT

Egg and Pork Rolls
Rolé derri e ftohtë

1 1/2 pounds boneless pork—preferably from ribs
Salt
Pepper
1 tablespoon chopped parsley
2 stalks celery, chopped
3 eggs, beaten and fried into an omelette
2 onions, sliced
2 carrots, sliced
1/2 pound pickles

Cut meat in a large rectangular sheet (1/2-inch thick) and beat thoroughly; season with salt, pepper, parsley and celery, and cover with an egg omelette prepared in advance. Roll meat and omelette together, wrap in a fine cambric, tie, and put in salted boiling water, together with onions and carrots. Boil until tender, rinse, remove wrapping and put in the fridge for a couple of hours. Cut in slices and serve cold, garnished with pickles or salad.
    4 servings.

Cheese Salad
Liptao

1 pound feta cheese (or cottage cheese, or drained yogurt)
5 tablespoons pure olive oil
5 garlic cloves, finely grated and crushed
2 tablespoons chopped pickled red peppers
Salt
Pepper

Pour feta cheese, or cottage cheese, or drained yogurt into a pan; add olive oil, garlic and pickled red peppers. Mix well until a compact mixture is obtained. Season with salt and pepper. Serve with olives around, in small dishes.

You can garnish the cheese salad with a few slices of mortadella, roastbeef, cucumber pickles (with no or very little sugar), carrots, a few sardines in olive oil, or boiled eggs, cut in halves.

4 servings.

Baked Eggplant Salad
Sallatë pure patëllxhani

2 pounds eggplant
10 garlic cloves, chopped
3 tablespoons chopped parsley
1/2 teacup pure olive oil
1/2 teacup vinegar
Salt
Pepper

Grill or bake the whole eggplants until tender. Peel eggplants and mash; mix well with garlic, parsley, olive oil, vinegar, salt and pepper in a porcelain or earthenware bowl. Serve cold in small dishes, sprinkling the salad with olive oil.

Serves 6.

Baked Peppers Salad
Sallatë me speca të pjekur

2 pounds bell peppers, preferably yellow
5 garlic cloves, crushed
1/2 cup olive oil
3 tablespoons vinegar
Salt
Pepper

Roast peppers and peel them. Remove stems and seeds and dice peppers. Add crushed garlic cloves, oil, vinegar, salt and pepper and mix well. Serve cold, in small dishes.
Serves 6.

Mashed Dried Beans Salad
Sallatë pure fasulesh

1 cup dried white beans
1/2 cup olive oil
2 tablespoons vinegar
1/4 cup crushed walnuts
5 garlic cloves, crushed
1 tablespoon chopped parsley
Salt
Pepper

Boil beans in a pressure cooker for 30 minutes, drain, mash and pass through a colander over a bowl. Stir in oil, vinegar, crushed nuts and garlic cloves, chopped parsley, salt and pepper. Lay the salad on a dish, flattening and undulating it with a spoon, and sprinkle with olive oil. Serve cold.
4 servings.

Chickory Salad
Sallatë radhiqe

1 1/2 pounds chickory leaves
1/4 cup olive oil
1/4 cup lemon juice

Choose young chickory leaves; cut off roots and wash them thoroughly. Leave in cold water for half an hour, then rinse several times. Let drain and put in boiling salted water for 10 minutes. Drain well, chop, and mix with oil and lemon juice in a bowl. Serve cold.
4 servings.

Spinach Purée and Cucumber Pickles
Pure spinaqi me tranguj turshi

2 pounds spinach
1 pound grated cucumber pickles
5 garlic cloves, finely grated
Chili powder
1/2 cup olive oil
4 tablespoons lemon juice

Put spinach in boiling salted water for 5 minutes; drain, squeeze, and purée in a blender. Put in a bowl and mix thoroughly with cucumber pickles, garlic, chili powder, olive oil and lemon juice.
Serves 6.

Spinach Salad
Sallatë spinaqi

2 pounds spinach
4 garlic cloves, crushed
1/2 cup olive oil
3 tablespoons vinegar

Wash spinach thoroughly and put it in boiling salted water for 3 minutes. Drain well, chop and mix with crushed garlic cloves, oil and vinegar.
Serves 6.

Radish Salad
Sallatë me rrepa të kuqe

2 pounds radishes
1 pound cucumber pickles, sliced
3 tablespoons vinegar
3 onions, sliced into rings
4 tablespoons drained plain yogurt
4 garlic cloves, crushed
Salt
Pepper
1/2 cup olive oil
1 tablespoon chopped parsley

Remove leaves and tips from radish roots, wash roots thoroughly and slice. Put them in the middle of a dish, mix with sliced cucumber pickles and vinegar, and cover with onion round slices. Garnish this mixture with drained yogurt mixed with crushed garlic cloves and salt and pepper, and sprinkle everything with oil and parsley.
Serves 6.

Mashed Potatoes Salad
Sallatë pure patatesh

1 pound potatoes
1/4 cup olive oil
3 tablespoons vinegar
6 garlic cloves, crushed
5 walnuts, chopped
Salt
Pepper

Wash and boil potatoes in salted water until tender. Drain, peel and mash potatoes. Put the mashed potatoes in an earthenware bowl and stir in oil, vinegar, crushed garlic cloves and walnuts, and salt and pepper. Flatten the mixture in a dish, undulating it with a spoon, and sprinkle with additional olive oil. Serve cold.
4 servings.

Beet Salad
Sallatë panxhari

2 pounds red beets
1 large orange
1/4 cup olive oil
1/4 cup vinegar
5 garlic cloves, crushed
Salt
Pepper

Remove leaves and tips from beet roots and boil them until tender. Peel, cut in half, and slice beets, and put in an earthenware bowl. Peel and slice the orange, and mix with the beet slices. Stir in oil, vinegar, garlic, salt and pepper. Serve cold.
4 servings.

Cauliflower Salad
Sallatë lulelakër

1 pound cauliflower
1/4 cup olive oil
Juice of 1 large lemon, or 3 tablespoons vinegar
Salt
Pepper

Remove leaves and stem from the cauliflower and boil it in salted water until tender. Drain and dice cauliflower, and combine with oil, lemon juice or vinegar, and salt and pepper. Serve cold.
4 servings.

Cabbage Salad
Sallatë me lakër

1 pound white cabbage
Salt
Pepper
Red pepper powder
1/4 cup olive oil
1/4 cup vinegar
1 teaspoon sugar
1 tablespoon chopped parsley

Wash cabbage thoroughly and shred it. Add salt, pepper and red pepper powder, and press down on the mixture with your hand until some juice is produced. Stir in oil, vinegar and sugar. Sprinkle with chopped parsley before serving.
4 servings.

Mushroom Salad
Sallatë këpurdhash

2 pounds mushrooms
1 teaspoon chopped dill
1/2 cup olive oil
5 tablespoons lemon juice, or 3 tablespoons vinegar
Salt

Boil mushrooms in boiling salted water. Drain, slice and sprinkle mushrooms with dill, oil, and lemon juice or vinegar. Add salt to taste. Serve cold.
Serves 6.

Yogurt Salad
Tarator

Salt
1 pound yogurt
1/2 pound cucumber, peeled and finely diced
3 garlic cloves, crushed
6 tablespoons olive oil, divided

Stir salt in yogurt and beat thoroughly. Add diced cucumber, crushed garlic cloves, and 2 tablespoons oil, and keep beating for a couple of minutes. Serve in small bowls, sprinkling each bowl with 1 tablespoon olive oil.
4 servings.

HOT DISHES
GJELLËT E NGROHTA

BROILED DISHES
TAVAT

Broiled Lamb and Yogurt
Tavë Kosi

For yogurt sauce:

1 1/2 pounds lamb
Salt
Pepper
4 tablespoons (1/2 stick) butter
2 tablespoons rice

1 tablespoon flour
4 tablespoons (1/2 stick) butter
2 pounds yogurt
Salt
Pepper
5 eggs

Cut meat in 4 serving pieces, sprinkle each piece with salt and pepper, and bake in a moderately heated oven with half of the butter, sprinkling the meat with its gravy now and then. When meat is half-baked, add rice; remove the baking pan from the oven and leave it aside while you prepare the yogurt sauce: Sauté flour in butter until mixed thoroughly. Mix yogurt with salt, pepper and eggs until a uniform mixture is obtained, and finally stir in the flour. Put the sauce mixture in the baking pan; stir it with the meat pieces and bake at 375°F for about 45 minutes. Serve hot.

4 servings.

Stuffed Lamb Breast
Gjoks qingji i mbushur

1/4 pound bread slices
1 cup milk
1/2 pound ground pork
2 fresh onions, chopped
3 tablespoons butter
6 garlic cloves, crushed
2 tablespoons chopped parsley
2 eggs
1 cup white wine
Salt
Pepper
1 1/2 pounds baby lamb breast
2 tablespoons oil

To make stuffing:

Immerse bread in milk for a minute, squeeze, and combine in a bowl with ground pork. Sauté onion in butter and add to the pork mixture together with the crushed garlic cloves, parsley, eggs, wine, salt and pepper. Mix everything thoroughly.

Make a pocket between meat and ribs of lamb breast and put in the stuffing. Sew closed the opening and put the meat in a baking dish. Season with salt and pepper, sprinkle with oil and bake for about 1 1/2 hours at 380°F. When well done, remove bones and thread. Slice into serving pieces and serve with mashed potatoes sprinkled with sauce prepared with the pan drippings.
4 servings.

Meat and Potatoes in Sauce
Mish me patate jahni

1 pound lamb, veal or pork
1 onion, chopped
5 garlic cloves, chopped
1/4 cup oil
3/4 cup red wine
1 tablespoon tomato sauce
1 tablespoon chopped parsley
1 teaspoon chopped celery
3 pounds potatoes, peeled and cut into 1/2-inch sticks
Salt
Pepper

Wash, drain and cut meat in four pieces. Sauté chopped onion and garlic cloves in oil for a few minutes, then add meat to the frying pan and sauté for another 10 minutes. Stir in wine and mix well. Add tomato sauce, parsley and celery; put everything in a casserole with a lid on top and cook for about 30 minutes at 300°F. Add potatoes, 3/4 cup hot water, and salt and pepper and cook until potatoes are tender. Serve hot.

4 servings.

Baked Leg of Lamb with Potatoes
Kofshë qingji me patate në furrë

1 1/2 pounds leg of lamb
1 large lemon, sliced
Salt
Pepper
2 pounds potatoes
6 tablespoons butter or margarine

Wash and dry meat, and rub thoroughly with lemon pieces. Season meat with salt and pepper and put in a baking pan. Peel, wash and cut potatoes, and place them around the meat. Add additional salt and pepper along with butter or margarine and bake at 375°F until tender, sprinkling the meat now and then with its own juice. Serve hot.
4 servings.

Baked Mutton
Mish dashi në gjyveç

4 tablespoons butter or margarine, divided
Salt
Pepper
Oregano
3 bay leaves
1 1/2 pounds mutton (leg or shoulder)
1 large onion, sliced
5 carrots, peeled and sliced
5 garlic cloves, chopped
1 cup red wine

Preheat oven to 350°F. Combine butter or margarine, salt, pepper, oregano and bay leaves. Spread half of the butter mixture in a roasting pan so that the bottom is covered thoroughly. Cut meat in 1/4-inch thick slices and spread half of them on top, then put remaining layer of butter mixture along with sliced onion, and finally add a second layer of meat slices.

Sauté sliced carrots and garlic cloves with some butter or margarine and put them on top of the meat. Add the red wine and 1/2 cup water, cover tightly and bake until tender. Serve hot, accompanied with mashed potatoes or French fries.

You can also cook this dish in a pressure cooker on the stove, in a shorter time, and with almost the same results.
4 servings.

Mutton or Pork with Vegetables
Mish dashi ose derri me perime

1 1/2 pounds mutton or pork
1/2 cup oil
1 large onion, grated
1 tablespoon tomato sauce
Salt
Pepper
1 pound potatoes, peeled and cut into chunks
1/2 pound pearl onions, peeled
1/2 pound carrots, peeled and cut into chunks
3 celery stalks, chopped
2 tablespoons chopped parsley
1 hot pepper, chopped
2 bay leaves

Cut meat in four pieces and sauté in hot oil until reddish. Remove meat from the frying pan and sauté grated onion. Add tomato sauce, 2 cups hot water, salt and pepper, and let simmer for half an hour. Sauté potatoes, onions, carrots, celery and parsley in a separate pan. Put sautéed vegetables in a casserole. Layer the meat slices over the vegetables. Pour tomato sauce mixture over meat. Add chopped hot pepper and the bay leaves, and then put the dish in the oven. Bake at 350°F until tender. Serve hot.

4 servings.

You can prepare this dish with other vegetables, depending on the season.

Wine-slaked Meat
Mish i shuar me verë

1/4 pound lard
1 1/2 pounds boneless meat (veal, mutton, pork)
Salt
Pepper
1/2 pound carrots, peeled and sliced
1 large onion, chopped
2 celery stalks, chopped
1 cup red wine
1 cup meat stock
1/2 pound kidney beans
1/2 pound green peas
4 tablespoons butter or margarine
4 garlic cloves, crushed
2 bay leaves
2 tablespoons chopped parsley

Cut lard in thin slices and fry in a saucepan. Season meat thoroughly with salt and pepper and sauté it in the saucepan with the melted lard. Add 1 cup of the carrots, along with the onion and celery and sauté them with the meat for 10 minutes. Drain the fat from the saucepan and pour wine and stock over the meat. Boil for about 1 hour over low heat, covered, until most of the juice evaporates and some gravy remains. Remove the meat and put it in a dish. Pass the gravy through a sieve and, if not thick enough, boil for a few minutes.

Boil kidney beans, peas, and remaining carrots in salted water for a few minutes, and then sauté in butter or margarine with garlic and bay leaves. Cut meat in thin slices and put 3 to 4 slices in each dish, with the vegetables around, then pour some sauce on top. Serve hot, garnished with chopped parsley.

4 servings.

Meat and Pearl Onions
Mish çomlek me qepë

1 1/2 pounds boneless meat
3/4 cup oil
Salt
Coarsely ground black pepper
Cinnamon
2 bay leaves
2 large onions, sliced in small squares
3 tablespoons vinegar
2 pounds pearl onions, pared
12 garlic cloves, crushed
1 cup tomato juice, or 2 tablespoons tomato sauce

Preheat oven to 350° F.

Cut meat in small pieces and brown thoroughly in a deep pot in very hot oil. Add salt, pepper, cinnamon, bay leaves and the sliced large onions, and fry everything until reddish. Stir in vinegar and 1/2 cup hot water.

Add pared small onions and garlic cloves, tomato juice or diluted tomato sauce in 1 cup water. Cover tightly and bake for about 2 hours until liquid has cooked away. Serve hot.

4 servings.

*You can use a pressure cooker for cooking fast (about 30 minutes) instead of baking.

Veal Head Stew
Paçe koke viçi

1 veal head
Salt
1 large onion, finely grated
2 celery stalks, chopped
5 garlic cloves, minced
2 tablespoons chopped parsley
1 pound various vegetables, diced
3 tablespoons vinegar
Pepper

Remove brain from head and wash head thoroughly. Put it in a pan, season with salt, and boil for 1 hour in 8 cups water. Remove head and let liquid boil until only half of it remains. Remove all meat from head, slice in small squares and return to the pan. Add grated onion, celery, garlic, parsley, and diced vegetables. Mix thoroughly and sprinkle with vinegar and pepper. Boil for another 15 minutes. Serve hot, with a salad.
4 servings.

Stuffed Rolled Veal Neck
Qafë viçi e mbushur rolé

2 pounds veal neck
Salt
Pepper
2 red peppers, sliced
5 garlic cloves, crushed
2 tablespoons chopped parsley
1 large onion
3 carrots

Remove all bones, tendons and membranes from the meat, giving it a rectangle form, and spread it on the table, the inside down. Beat thoroughly and sprinkle with salt and pepper. Spread squarely sliced peppers, crushed garlic and chopped parsley over meat and roll up. Tie with a piece of string. Cut onion and carrots in a few pieces and put them together with the rolled meat in an oiled pan. Season meat with salt and pepper and put the pan in the oven. Bake at 375°F , sprinkling now and then with juice obtained from boiling the bones, until tender and well-browned. When done, remove string, cut in slices, sprinkle with gravy and serve hot with French fries and salad.

4 servings.

Veal and Okra
Mish viçi me bamje

1 1/2 pounds okra
Salt
1/2 cup vinegar
1/2 cup oil, divided
1 1/2 pounds veal
2 onions, grated
1/2 pound tomatoes, sliced
1 tablespoon chopped parsley
Pepper

Remove the cone-shaped caps of okras by cutting a thin coniform slice, and wash them. Sprinkle with salt and vinegar and leave them aside for an hour. Sauté in 1/4 cup oil until yellowish. Cut meat in 4 pieces, salt and sauté together with onion in remaining oil. Add sliced tomatoes and 1/2 cup water and cook over low heat for 30 minutes. Add okra, salt, parsley, pepper, cover tightly and cook until a thick gravy remains. Serve hot.

4 servings.

Meat and White Beans
Mish me fasule

1 pound mutton, pork, bacon, or corned beef, chopped
1/2 cup oil, divided
1 pound white beans
Salt
1 cup grated onion
2 carrots, grated
2 tablespoons tomato sauce
Red pepper powder
Mint

Sauté chopped meat in 1/4 cup oil until brown. Wash and boil beans for 5 minutes in a stock pot. Rinse beans and boil again, together with meat in 2 cups water for about 2 hours in the pot or for about 30 minutes in a pressure cooker until tender, then add salt. Sauté onion in remaining oil until yellowish, add carrots and sauté for a few minutes, then stir in tomato sauce, red pepper, salt and mint to taste. Add this mixture in the pot and let boil for a few minutes with the beans. Serve hot, with pickles.
Serves 4.

Lamb entrails
Të brendshme qingji jahni

1 1/2 pounds lamb entrails
3 large onions, sliced into half circles
1/2 cup oil
1 tablespoon flour
1 cup red wine
1/4 cup vinegar
3 large tomatoes, chopped
6 garlic cloves, finely grated
2 bay leaves
Salt
Pepper

Clean and wash entrails with boiling water, rinse and cut in 1-inch squares. Sauté onions in oil. Add entrails and sauté for a few minutes. Add flour, sauté until yellow. Stir in wine and vinegar, add tomatoes, garlic and laurel leaves, and cook over medium heat, covered, until meat is well done. Stir in salt and pepper. Serve hot.
   4 servings.

Pork and Cauliflower
Mish derri me lulelakër

1 1/2 pounds pork
1/4 cup oil
1/2 cup grated onion
1/2 cup grated carrots
1 tablespoon tomato sauce
1 tablespoon chopped parsley
1 teaspoon chopped celery
2 pounds cauliflower
Salt
Pepper

   Cut meat in four portions and sauté in oil together with grated onion and carrots in a pot, until brownish. Add tomato sauce diluted with water, parsley and celery and 1 cup hot water. Cook for half an hour. Wash the cauliflower, dip in boiling salted water for 1 minute, drain and cut in small pieces, and add to the meat. Cook until tender. Season with salt and pepper to taste. Serve hot.
   4 servings.

GROUND MEAT
MISHI I GRIRË

Ground meat is widely used in Albanian cooking to prepare a variety of dishes, ranging from meatballs—*qofte*—to soups. We have chosen a few recipes which we feel are representative of the best in Albanian cooking. You can use all kinds of ground meat—veal, beef, lamb, pork, as well as a variety of spices.

Barbecued Meatballs
Qofte të skarës

1/4 pound stale bread
1 pound finely ground meat (a mixture of 70% beef or veal
    and 30% pork is recommended)
2 tablespoons bread crumbs
2 tablespoons oil or butter
Salt
Pepper
1 small onion, finely grated
1 tablespoon chopped parsley
Oregano

Soak bread in water and squeeze hard to drain. Add ground meat, bread crumbs, oil or melted butter, salt, pepper, onion, parsley, and oregano. Mix thoroughly, and make into 1-inch thick sausages. Sprinkle with salt, pepper and oregano, and barbecue. Serve hot with French fries or mashed potatoes.
    4 servings.

Fried Meatballs
Qofte të fërguara

1 pound ground meat
1 slice stale bread
2 tablespoons chopped feta cheese
1 onion, finely grated
Salt
Pepper
Mint
1/2 cup flour
1 cup oil

Combine the first 7 ingredients as in the above recipe. Form mixture into 1/2-inch thick patties or sausages. Roll in flour and fry in hot oil. Serve hot with French fries or mashed potatoes.
4 servings.

Meatballs in Sauce
Qofte me salcë

3 tablespoons tomato sauce
3 tablespoons butter
Salt
2 bay leaves
3 tablespoons vinegar
1 1/2 pounds ground meat
1 slice stale bread

3 onions
3 eggs
Pepper
Mint
3 tablespoons flour
1 cup oil

Dilute tomato sauce in 1/4 cup water. Stir in butter, salt, bay leaves, and vinegar, and cook for about 20 minutes over medium heat. Mix the meat, bread, onions, eggs, pepper, and mint as in the above recipe. Form mixture into meatballs or sausages, roll in flour and fry in oil.

Add meatballs in the pot with the sauce.Cook over low heat, covered, for a few minutes. Serve hot with mashed potatoes. 4 servings.

Meatballs in Cream Sauce
Qofte me salcë të bardhë

1/2 cup rice
1 pound ground meat
2 onions, finely grated
4 tablespoons butter
3 eggs, separated
1 tablespoon chopped parsley
Salt
Pepper
Juice of 1 large lemon
2 tablespoons flour
1 cup milk

Boil rice for 10 minutes, drain, and mix with meat in a bowl. Sauté onion in butter in a saucepan and add to meat mixture together with the whites of the eggs, finely chopped parsley, and salt and pepper. Mix thoroughly and make into 1-inch round balls, and sauté in the remaining butter. Stir lemon juice in a pot with 2 cups boiling salted water, add meatballs and cook for about 20 minutes over moderate heat.

Prepare a thin creamy sauce: sauté flour in the remaining butter, mixing continuously until yellowish and well blended. Season with salt and pepper and stir in small amounts of hot milk, mixing continuously over low heat until it starts boiling. Remove saucepan from heat and add egg yolks, stirring continuously. When ready, stir sauce in the caserole and heat to simmering. Serve hot, sprinkled with chopped parsley.

4 servings.

Baked Meatballs and Onions
Qofte të furrës me qepë

1 1/2 pounds ground meat	2 pounds onions
2 slices stale bread	6 garlic cloves, finely grated
3 egg whites	2 tablespoons tomato sauce
Pepper	4 tablespoons vinegar
1/2 cup flour	3 bay leaves
1 cup oil	Salt

Preheat oven to 375°F.

Prepare meatballs: Mix the meat, bread, eggwhites, and pepper. Form mixture into 1/2-inch thick sausages, roll in flour, and fry in oil. Cut onions in half-circle slices, sauté in the remaining oil, add grated garlic, tomato sauce, vinegar, bay leaves, 1/4 cup water, salt and pepper, cook until a thick sauce is obtained. Put meatballs in a baking dish, cover with the sauce and bake for about 20 minutes. Serve hot.

4 servings.

Meatballs and Walnuts
Qofte me arra

2 pounds ground meat
2 tablespoons flour
2 eggs
1 onion, finely grated
6 garlic cloves, finely grated
2 tablespoons chopped parsley
Salt
Pepper
1 cup oil
1/2 cup wine
1/2 cup peeled walnuts

Mix ground meat with 1 tablespoon flour, then add eggs, grated onion and garlic, parsley, salt and pepper. Mix thoroughly and make into 1-inch round balls. Sauté meatballs in hot oil until done and reserve them in another saucepan. Sauté 1 tablespoon flour in the remaining oil until brownish. Stir in wine and 1 cup water, cook for a few minutes, then pour over the meatballs in the saucepan and simmer for 5 minutes. Crush or grind walnuts, mix with a small amount of water and stir in the saucepan. Cook for another 15 minutes. Serve hot.

4 servings.

Meatballs and Yogurt
Qofte me kos

1/4 cup rice
1 pound ground meat
1 onion, finely grated
1 tablespoon finely chopped parsley
1 tablespoon finely chopped dill
Salt
Pepper
2 tablespoons flour
1/2 cup oil
2 tablespoons tomato sauce
1 1/2 pounds yogurt
3 garlic cloves, finely grated or crushed

Put rice in boiling water for 5 minutes, drain and mix well with meat, onion, parsley, dill, salt and pepper. Make into cigar-shaped meatballs. Sauté flour in oil, add sauce, 2 cups water and cook for a few minutes. Add meatballs and cook for another 45 minutes, until a thick gravy remains.

Serve cold, covered with tomato sauce and yogurt beaten with finely grated garlic cloves and seasoned with salt.

4 servings.

Lamb Entrails Sausages
Llukanikë me të brendshme qingji

1 1/2 pounds lamb entrails
1/2 pound lamb or veal intestines
12 garlic cloves
1 tablespoon red pepper
1 teaspoon hot red pepper
1 tablespoon chopped oregano
1 tablespoon chopped dill
1/2 teaspoon grated nutmeg
Salt
Pepper

Pass lamb entrails and intestines together with garlic cloves through the meat grinder 3 times. Put the mixture in a bowl and add all the other ingredients. Wash, drain and let intestines dry. Attach an end of the intestine to the special funnel-shaped attachment of the grinder, fill the grinder with the mixture and start turning its handle to fill the intestine; every 3 to 4 inches stop the grinder, give the intestine a twist, and keep filling the intestine until all mixture is used, and a chain of sausages is formed. Pierce sausages with a needle and put them in boiling salted water for a couple of minutes. Hang over stove and let dry for 3 days. Keep in the fridge.
Serves 6.

POULTRY and RABBIT
SHPENDËT, LEPURI

Chicken and Rice (Pilau)
Pulë me pilaf

1 chicken (1 1/2 pounds)
4 tablespoons butter, divided
4 tablespoons flour
1/2 cup milk
2 egg yolks
Salt
Pepper
2 cups rice

Bring chicken to a boil, skim as necessary and boil for 15 minutes over low heat, in 5 to 7 cups water, depending on the variety of rice. Save 1 cup of stock to prepare the sauce. Remove chicken from water, cut in 4 serving pieces and sauté in 2 tablespoons butter. Set aside chicken pieces and sauté flour in the remaining butter. Add milk and 1 cup of reserved stock, mixing continuously to avoid lumps from forming. Leave aside to cool, then add egg yolks, salt and pepper, mixing continuously, until a white sauce is formed.

Bring the remaining juice to boil and add rice, salt and 2 tablespoons butter. Simmer over low heat until all juice is absorbed and the pilau is well done.

Serve hot, smothering chicken pieces with sauce.

4 servings.

Chicken and Walnuts
Pulë me arra

1 chicken (1 1/2 pounds)
4 tablespoons butter, divided
2 tablespoons flour
1 cup peeled walnuts
2 tablespoons vinegar
6 garlic cloves, crushed
Salt
Pepper

Simmer chicken in 6 cups salted water until tender (about 2 hours). Reserve 1 cup of stock. Remove chicken from water, cut in 4 portions and sauté in 2 tablespoons butter. Use the remaining 2 tablespoons butter to sauté flour, then stir in the stock mixing continuously to avoid lumps from forming. When it starts to boil, add walnuts, vinegar, garlic, salt and pepper and cook for a few minutes. Serve hot with the chicken pieces.
4 servings.

Stuffed Chicken
Pulë e mbushur

1 onion, chopped
4 tablespoons butter
1/2 pound ground veal
1 young chicken (1 1/2 pounds), entrails included
1 cup white wine, divided
1/2 pound tomatoes, finely sliced, divided
Salt
Pepper
Cinnamon
1 tablespoon bread crumbs
1 lemon slice

Preheat oven to 350°F.

Sauté onion in butter, and then add ground veal and chopped chicken entrails and continue to sauté. Stir in half of wine, then add half of tomatoes, salt, pepper, cinnamon, and 1 cup water and cook for about 1/2 hour. Stir in bread crumbs. Fill the chicken with this mixture, sew, rub with a slice of lemon, season with salt and pepper and sauté on all sides in 2 table-spoons butter.

Add the remaining wine and tomatoes and bake, sprinkling now and then with the gravy, for about 1 hour. When well done, remove the stuffing and slice into serving pieces.

4 servings.

Chicken and White Sauce
Pulë frikasé

1 young chicken (1 1/2 pounds)
3 onions, chopped
4 tablespoons butter
3 tablespoons flour
Salt
Pepper
2 egg yolks
1 lemon
1 tablespoon chopped parsley

Bring chicken to a boil, cook for a few minutes, remove from the pan, drain (reserve 1 cup of stock), season with salt and pepper and cut in 4 portions. Sauté chicken and onions in butter until yellowish. Add flour, mixing continously for a few minutes, then stir in reserved stock until chicken is covered completely. Add salt and pepper, cover and boil over low heat until a thick gravy is obtained.

Turn heat off and wait a few minutes. Beat yolks in lemon juice, then add to gravy, mixing continuously until a white sauce is obtained. Stir in parsley before serving. Serve hot, over chicken.
    4 servings.

Baked Chicken and Vegetables
Pulë e pjekur me perime

1 young chicken (1 1/2 pounds)
Salt
Pepper
6 tablespoons butter, divided
1 onion, chopped
1 cup white wine
1/2 pound tomatoes, peeled and sliced
1/2 pound peas
1/2 pound carrots, sliced
1 pound potatoes, sliced
2 tablespoons chopped parsley

Cut chicken in 4 to 5 serving pieces, season with salt and pepper and sauté in 4 tablespoons butter. Add onion and sauté. Add wine, a bit of water and tomatoes, and bake for 1/2 hour at 375°F. In the meantime put peas in boiling water for a couple of minutes, sauté carrots in 2 tablespoons butter and add these to the baking pan.
    Sauté potatoes in the remaining butter and add to the baking pan; add parsley, salt, pepper and a bit of water as necessary. Cover tightly and bake for 1 additional hour. Serve hot.
    4 servings.

Chicken, Spinach and Yogurt
Pulë me spinaq e kos

2 pounds young chicken, in serving pieces
4 tablespoons butter
1 onion, finely grated
Salt
Pepper
2 cups yogurt
1 tablespoon flour
3 pounds spinach, chopped

Sauté chicken pieces in butter and put in a baking pan. Sprinkle with onion, salt and pepper, add a bit of water and bake for 1 hour at 375°F. Mix yogurt with a bit water, flour and salt in a bowl and add to the baking pan. Bake for another 1/2 hour. Boil spinach in salted water for a few minutes, drain and serve with meat on top, covered with the yogurt sauce.
4 servings.

Goose and Oranges
Patë me portokaj

1 young goose
Salt
Pepper
1 lemon, cut into slices
4 tablespoons butter
1 pound oranges
1 tablespoon flour

Season goose inside with salt and pepper, and rub the out-side with lemon slices. Season with salt and pepper, coat with butter and bake for about 2 hours at 375°F. Meanwhile, wash oranges, grate off the outer layer of rind, peel them and slice the rind. Put sliced rind in boiling water for a couple of minutes, drain and put in cold water. Peel pulp and remove seeds. Combine flour, butter and drippings, to prepare a brown sauce and pour half of it on top of the orange pulp. Cut baked goose in serving pieces and serve hot, covered with a mixture of sauce and sliced rind, with orange pulp around.

4 servings.

Turkey and Chestnut Dressing
Gjeldeti i mbushur me gështenja

1 onion, finely grated
6 tablespoons butter, divided
Turkey entrails, sliced
1 cup milk
2 pounds chestnuts, unshelled
1/4 cup raisins
Cinnamon
Salt
Pepper
4 tablespoons bread crumbs
1 young turkey
1 lemon, sliced

Sauté onion in 2 tablespoons butter; add entrails; sauté, and add milk and simmer for 1 hour. Boil unshelled chestnuts for 20 minutes, drain, shell and peel off brown skin while hot. Add chestnuts to the entrails and bring to a boil. Add raisins, cinnamon, 2 tablespoons butter, salt and pepper and mix thoroughly. Add bread crumbs to absorb all liquid and remove from heat. Stuff turkey with this mixture, sew and rub the

whole surface with lemon slices. Sprinkle with salt and pepper, cover with the remaining butter and bake for about 3 hours at 350°F. When well done remove stuffing and cut meat in 8 serving pieces. Serve hot with French fries and sauce prepared with the remaining drippings.
Serves 8.

Grouse and Olives
Thëllëzë me ullinj

4 grouse
3 tablespoons flour
5 tablespoons butter, divided
1 cup white wine
1 cup gravy
Salt
Pepper
1 tablespoon chopped parsley
1/2 pound tomatoes, chopped
1/2 pound olives
Chicory salad (recommended)

Cut each grouse in half, dredge the pieces in 2 tablespoons flour, and sauté over medium heat in 3 tablespoons butter until lightly brown on both sides. Add wine. Sauté 1 tablespoon flour in 2 tablespoons butter in a saucepan, add gravy, and mix thoroughly. Add salt, pepper, parsley and tomatoes and simmer for 15 minutes until the sauce is well blended and slightly thickened.

Seed the olives and boil for a few minutes to remove salt. Drain olives and mix with meat and sauce and simmer for another 10 minutes. Serve hot, preferably with chicory salad.
4 servings.

Rabbit and Onions
Lepur çomlek

3 pounds rabbit, cut into serving pieces
1/2 cup vinegar
Pepper
Oregano
1 tablespoon chopped parsley
2 cloves
2 bay leaves
1/2 cup oil
5 tomatoes, peeled and chopped
10 garlic cloves, crushed
3 pounds small onions, peeled
Salt

Marinate rabbit before cooking: put rabbit pieces in an earthenware bowl with vinegar, water, pepper, oregano, parsley, cloves and bay leaves. Cover everything with a heavy lid so that meat pieces immerse completely and let marinate for about 12 hours.

Drain meat, squeeze and sauté in hot oil. Add a little vinegar, a bit of water, tomatoes, garlic cloves, and cook over low heat for 1 hour. Sauté onions, put them together with the other ingredients in a baking pan, season with salt and pepper, cover tightly and bake for 1 hour at 350°F. Serve hot.

You can also prepare this dish with hare or wild boar following the same procedure.

4 servings.

VEGETABLES
PERIMET

Vegetables are widely used in Albanian cooking. Plenty of excellent and simple methods of cooking them are available, with or without any meat. The cooking methods recommended in the following pages have been summarized under each vegetable, to make it easier for the reader. A good cooking method should meet the following requirements in order to keep nutritive losses to a minimum:

To prevent loss of vitamin C, contact with air should be avoided:

—by leaving the vegetables unpeeled;

—by displacing air in the untensil with steam;

—by covering cut surfaces with oil.

To destroy enzymes quickly, the initial heating must be rapid. Enzymes bring about the destruction of the vitamins.

To prevent almost all nutritive losses vegetables should be cooked the shortest time necessary to produce tenderness, and all liquid which touches them should be used; vegetables to be cut should be first thoroughly chilled.

If steaming is done without pressure, vegetables should be left uncut and unpeeled whenever possible.

Sautéing is a good method of cooking vegetables in their own juices; 2 to 3 tablespoons of hot fat need be used, so that all cut surfaces can be sealed from air, direct contact with water can be prevented and juices can be sealed in. It is important to drain and dry vegetables well before sautéing. This procedure is more like cooking without water rather than frying.

When frying, vegetables should first be thoroughly chilled. If the frying pan is covered, contact with air is prevented by fat and steam, the vegetables cook in their own juices, cooking time is short and initial heating is rapid. A wide variety of vegetables are more delicious when fried.

Baking as a method of cooking vegetables is far superior to boiling, although vitamin C is not well preserved, because of long cooking and slow initial heating. Anyway, if vegetables are to be sliced and baked, the water should be hot, the oven preheated and the casserole tightly covered, to hold steam in.

ARTICHOKES

Stuffed Artichokes
Angjinare të mbushura

3 pounds artichokes
1 cup finely grated onion
1 pound ground meat
2 garlic cloves, crushed
1/2 cup olive oil
1 pound tomatoes, peeled and chopped
3 bay leaves
Salt
Pepper
Basil
Dill
1 tablespoon butter
2 tablespoons grated cheese

Cut off inedible tips of artichokes and boil for 5 minutes in salty water. Sauté onion, meat and garlic in olive oil. Add tomatoes and sauté. Add bay leaves, salt, pepper, dill and basil, and stuff this mixture between artichoke leaves. Sprinkle with butter and cheese, and bake for 45 minutes at 350°F. Serve hot.
4 servings.

Artichokes in Mayonnaise
Angjinare me majonezë

3 pounds artichokes
1/2 teaspoon tartaric acid
Salt
Pepper
Dill
1 cup mayonnaise
Juice of 1 lemon
1 tablespoon olive oil
1 clove garlic, grated
1 tablespoon chopped parsley

Cut off inedible tips of artichokes and put them in salty water with tartaric acid for 30 minutes. Drain and steam under cover for 30 minutes or until tender. Sprinkle with salt, pepper and dill and serve cold, with mayonnaise, sprinkled with lemon juice, olive oil, grated garlic, and chopped parsley.
4 servings.

CABBAGE

Stuffed Cabbage Leaves
Dollma me mish të grirë

1 cabbage (about 3 pounds)
1/2 cup minced onion
1/2 cup oil
1/2 cup rice
1 pound ground meat
2 teaspoons tomato sauce, divided
Salt
Pepper
1 tablespoon flour
2 tablespoons butter
2 bay leaves
1 tablespoon chopped parsley

Cut off cabbage stalk and boil in hot water for 10 minutes. Sauté onion lightly in oil. Add washed rice and meat and sauté for a few minutes. Add 1 teaspoon tomato sauce, 1/4 cup water, salt, pepper and cook until all moisture evaporates. Put 1 tablespoon of this filling on one end of each cabbage leaf, roll, fold corners over the filling, roll again and fold corners up to the end of the leaf. Arrange these bundles in a deep saucepan tightly one against the other, on top of a layer of flat cabbage leaves, cover with a heavy dish, add as much salty water as needed to cover the bundles to about 3/4 of their depth. Cover tightly and cook over low heat for about 30 minutes or until almost all liquid has cooked away and leaves and filling are tender.

Sauté flour in butter in a frying pan. Add 1 teaspoon tomato sauce, salt, pepper, bay leaves and a bit of water and boil for a few minutes. Pour this sauce on top of the bundles and keep cooking for another 15 minutes. Serve hot, sprinkled with chopped parsley.

You can prepare this dish using grape leaves instead of cabbage leaves. The procedure is exactly the same.

4 servings.

CAULIFLOWER

Cauliflower and Milk
Lulelakër me qumësht

2 pounds cauliflower
2 eggs
1/2 cup milk
3 tablespoons grated cheddar cheese
2 tablespoons butter
1 tablespoon flour
Salt
Pepper

Boil cauliflower in salty water for 10 minutes or until tender. Break into florets and put in a baking pan brushed with melted butter. Mix beaten eggs with hot milk, and cover cauliflowers with this mixture. Sprinkle with cheese, butter and flour. Season with salt and pepper and bake in hot oven at 400°F for about 15 minutes. Serve hot.
4 servings.

Fried Cauliflower and Eggs
Lulelakër e skuqur me vezë

2 pounds cauliflower
1/2 cup grated cheddar cheese
Salt
Pepper
3 eggs
3 tablespoons flour
1/2 cup oil

Boil cauliflower in salty water for about 10 minutes or until just tender. Break into florets and drain. Sprinkle with cheese, salt and pepper. Beat eggs and mix with flour. Roll cauliflower florets in egg mixture and fry in oil. Serve hot.
4 servings.

DRIED BEANS

Dried Beans Jahni
Fasule jahni

2 cups dried white beans
1/2 cup chopped onion
1/2 cup oil
2 tablespoons tomato sauce

1 tablespoon chopped parsley
Salt
Chili powder
1 tablespoon chopped mint

Boil beans for 5 minutes in hot water. Rinse and boil for another 15 minutes in a covered stock pot in 3 cups hot water. Sauté onion in oil until yellow. Add 2 tablespoons bean stock from the pot, tomato sauce, parsley, salt and chili powder to taste. Cook for 10 minutes or until a thick sauce is formed, then pour it into the pot. Add chopped mint, cover tightly and cook for 2 hours over low heat, or for 30 minutes in a pressure cooker. This dish should produce a thick juice, covering beans 1/2 inch deep. Serve hot.

4 servings.

Baked Lima Beans
Fasule pllaqi

2 cups lima beans
2 large onions, sliced
3/4 cup olive oil
1 cup sliced carrots
3 garlic cloves, crushed
1 tablespoon chopped celery
2 tomatoes, sliced
Salt
Pepper

Boil beans in hot water for 15 minutes. Rinse and boil for another 30 minutes in 1 cup hot water. Sauté onion in oil until yellow. Add carrots and sauté for a few minutes. Add garlic, celery, tomato, salt, and pepper. Mix lightly and pour this mixture on top of beans in a baking pan. Bake for 1 hour at 350°F, or until almost all moisture has evaporated. Serve hot.

4 servings.

EGGPLANT

Stuffed Eggplant
Patëllxhane të mbushura

3 pounds small or medium–sized Italian eggplant
2 cups oil
2 pounds onions, chopped
20 garlic cloves, crushed
1 pound ground meat
1 pound tomatoes, chopped
1/4 cup vinegar
3 bay leaves
2 tablespoons chopped parsley
Salt
Pepper

Cut off stalks, and cut off 3 straps of peel 1/2 inch wide and scoop out almost half of the pulp from the eggplant. Soak eggplant in salty water for 30 minutes, drain, squeeze and sauté in 1 cup oil until lightly brown. Drain eggplant on paper towels. Use for a few minutes and use the remaining oil to sauté onion, garlic cloves and ground meat. Add tomatoes, vinegar, bay leaves, parsley, salt and pepper, then cook for 20 minutes or until meat is tender and almost all moisture has cooked away. Stuff eggplant with meat filling. Lay eggplant in 1 or 2 layers on the baking pan with the open side facing up. Put a few tomato slices on top of eggplant and bake for 1 hour at 375°F or until they are browned.
4 servings.

Eggplant Musaka
Musaka patëllxhani

3 pounds eggplant
1 1/2 cups oil, divided
1 cup chopped onions
1 pound ground meat
1 cup chopped tomatoes
1 tablespoon chopped parsley
Salt
Pepper
2 tablespoons bread crumbs

For the bechamel sauce:

2 tablespoons flour
3 tablespoons butter
1 cup hot milk
2 tablespoons grated cheese
1 egg yolk

Sauté flour in butter mixing continuously until yellowish. Stir in hot milk mixing rapidly. Bring to a boil, and turn heat off. Add cheese and yolk and keep mixing until well blended.

Cut eggplant slantwise in 1/4 inch slices, sauté in 1/2 cup oil and drain. Sauté onion and ground meat in the remaining oil, then add tomatoes, parsley, salt and pepper, and cook for a few minutes over moderate heat.

Brush bottom of baking pan with oil, sprinkle with bread crumbs, and then layer eggplant slices and meat mixture alternately, ending with eggplant slices. Cover with bechamel sauce, sprinkle with butter and bake for 1 hour at 375°F.

Serve hot.

4 servings.

Eggplant Stuffed with Cottage Cheese
Patëllxhane të mbushura me gjizë

3 pounds small or medium-sized eggplant
1/2 cup olive oil
4 eggs
1 cup salted cottage cheese
1 tablespoon chopped parsley
Salt

Cut off stalks, cut off 3 straps of peel 1/2 inch wide and scoop out 1/4 of the pulp from the eggplant. Soak eggplant in salty water for 30 minutes, drain, squeeze, and sauté in oil. Beat eggs in a bowl, and add cottage cheese, parsley and salt, and stuff this dressing into the eggplant. Bake for 1 hour at 375°F. Serve cold.
4 servings.

GREEN BEANS

Green Beans Jahni
Barbunja jahni

2 pounds green beans
1 cup chopped onions
1/2 pound ground meat
1/2 cup oil
1 cup diced tomatoes
1 tablespoon chopped parsley
Salt
Pepper

Cut off tips from both ends of beans and wash. Sauté onion and ground meat in oil. Add green beans in 4 to 5 batches and sauté under cover until cooked and almost all moisture has evaporated. Add tomato, as much water as needed to cover beans, parsley, salt and pepper, and cook over low heat until all moisture has cooked away. Serve hot.

4 servings.

LEEKS

Baked Leeks
Tavë me presh

2 pounds leeks
1/2 cup oil
3/4 cup chopped onions
1/2 pound ground meat
1 cup beef stock
1 tablespoon tomato sauce
Mild red pepper
Salt
Pepper

Cut off the green leaves from leeks; wash and cut leeks slantwise in 1-inch thick slices. Sauté in a little oil and put in a baking pan. Sauté onion and ground meat in the remaining oil. Add beef stock, tomato sauce, red pepper, salt and pepper, and bring to a boil. Pour meat mixture over sautéed leeks. Bake for 1 hour at 375°F. Serve hot.

4 servings.

Leek Musaka
Musaka me presh

3 pounds leeks
3/4 cup oil
1 cup grated onions
1 pound ground meat
1 tablespoon tomato sauce
1 tablespoon chopped parsley
2 bay leaves
Salt
Pepper
1/2 cup bread crumbs

For the bechamel sauce:

1 cup milk
2 eggs
3 tablespoons butter or margarine
3 tablespoons grated cheese
3 tablespoons flour

Cut off the green leaves from leeks, wash and cut them slantwise in 1-inch pieces. Sauté leeks in a little oil. Remove leeks, sauté onion in the remaining oil. Add meat and sauté until moisture cooks away. Add tomato sauce diluted in a bit of water, parsley, bay leaves, salt and pepper, and cook this stuffing until meat is tender.

Put one layer of leek pieces on the bottom of the baking pan sprinkled with oil and bread crumbs. Cover with a layer of meat mixture. Put another layer of leek pieces and cover everything with bechamel sauce (see *Eggplant Musaka* for the procedure, p. 56), sprinkle with cheese, butter or margarine and bake for 1 hour at 375°F. Serve hot.

4 servings.

Leeks in White Sauce
Presh me salcë të bardhë

3 pounds leeks
3/4 cup oil
1 cup grated onion
3 eggs
1 cup milk
Salt
Pepper
1/4 cup lemon juice

Cut off green leaves from leeks, and wash and cut them slantwise in 1-inch pieces. Lightly sauté leek pieces in a little oil, and remove them from the saucepan. Sauté onion in the remaining oil. Add leek pieces and 1/2 cup water, season with salt, and cook until half of the moisture has cooked away. Beat eggs in a bowl, mix with hot milk and leek stock until a white sauce is obtained. Pour the sauce on top of leeks in separate plates. Sprinkle with salt, pepper and lemon juice. Serve hot.
4 servings.

MIXED VEGETABLES

Macedoine of Vegetables
Turli perimesh

2 pounds various vegetables (peppers, potatoes, eggplants, okra, zucchini, etc.)
1/2 cup oil, divided
1 cup chopped onion
1 cup peeled chopped tomatoes
1 tablespoon chopped parsley
Salt
Pepper

Cut off inedible tips of vegetables, and wash and slice them into 1-inch squares. Sauté vegetables in half of the oil and remove them from the frying pan. Sauté onion and tomatoes in the remaining oil, and season with parsley, salt and pepper. Put everything in a stock pot with a cup of water, cover tightly, and simmer until almost all moisture has cooked away.

Serve hot, accompanied with steak, meatballs, or any other main dish.

4 servings.

MUSHROOMS

Baked Mushrooms
Tavë me këpurdha

3 pounds mushrooms
1 cup chopped onion
1/2 cup olive oil
1 tablespoon flour
1 tablespoon tomato sauce
Salt
Pepper
Dill

Put mushrooms in boiling salty water for 1 minute, drain and slice. Sauté onion in olive oil and add flour; sauté lightly. Add mushrooms, tomato sauce and 1 cup hot water. Season with salt, pepper, and dill, mix thoroughly, and put in a baking pan and bake in hot oven at 400°F for 15 minutes. Serve hot.

4 servings.

Mushroom Jahni
Këpurdha jahni

3 pounds mushrooms
1/2 cup oil
1 cup finely grated onion
6 garlic cloves, finely grated
1 tablespoon lemon juice
Salt
1 tablespoon chopped parsley

Boil mushrooms in boiling salty water for 1 minute, drain, slice and sauté in oil. Remove mushrooms and sauté onion until yellow, then add a little water and cook covered for a few minutes. Add mushrooms, garlic and lemon juice, and cook for another 5 minutes. Season with salt and sprinkle with parsley. Serve hot.
4 servings.

OKRA

Baked Okra
Tavë me bamje

2 pounds okra
Salt
1/4 cup vinegar
3/4 cup oil
1 pound tomatoes, peeled and chopped (divided)
1 cup chopped onions
1 pound ground meat
Pepper
Parsley

Remove the cone-shaped caps of okra by cutting a thin conic slice. Wash okra, sprinkle with salt and vinegar, and set aside for 20 minutes. Sauté okra in oil until yellowish. Cover the bottom of a baking pan with about half of the chopped tomatoes. Add sautéed okra to pan over layer of tomatoes. Sauté onion and meat in the remaining oil, add remaining tomatoes and sauté until meat is browned. Season meat mixture with salt and pepper. Add meat mixture over okra in baking pan, sprinkle with parsley, and bake for 1 hour at 375°F. Serve hot.

4 servings.

PEAS

Peas in White Sauce
Bizele me salcë të bardhë

2 pounds peas
1 tablespoon flour
2 tablespoons butter
2 cups milk
Salt
Pepper
Dill

Cook peas in boiling water for 5 minutes and drain. Sauté flour lightly in butter. Add milk, mixing continuously to avoid lumps from forming. Add peas and cook for another 5 minutes. Season with salt, pepper and dill. Serve hot.

4 servings.

Peas and Ground Meat
Bizele me mish të grirë

1 bunch scallions, green and white parts divided and chopped
1/2 cup oil
1/2 pound ground meat
2 pounds peas
1/2 tablespoon flour
1 teaspoon tomato sauce
Salt
Pepper
Dill

Sauté the white part of the scallions in oil. Add ground meat and continue to sauté. Cook peas in boiling water for 5 minutes, drain and sauté with scallions and meat. Add chopped green part of scallions, flour, tomato sauce, salt, pepper, dill and cook for 15 minutes. Serve hot.
4 servings.

PEPPERS

Stuffed Green Peppers
Speca të mbushur

12 green peppers
1/2 cup oil
1 pound onions, chopped
1 pound ground meat
1 pound tomatoes, chopped
Salt
Pepper
1/2 cup rice
Parsley
2 tomatoes, sliced
1 cup beef stock

Cut off stalks and scoop out seeds from peppers. Sauté the peppers lightly in oil and arrange in a baking pan. Sauté onion and meat in the remaining oil, and add chopped tomatoes. Season with salt and pepper, stir in 1 cup water and simmer for 15 minutes. Add rice and parsley, simmer for 10 minutes and remove from heat. Stuff this dressing into the peppers, cover with tomato slices, sprinkle with more salt, pepper and parsley, pour beef stock over them and bake for 1 hour at 375°F. Serve hot.

4 servings.

Fried Peppers and *Fërgesë*
Fërgesë me speca

2 pounds green peppers
3/4 cup olive oil
2 pounds tomatoes, peeled and grated
5 eggs
1/2 pound cottage cheese
6 garlic cloves, finely grated
Fresh chopped parsley
Salt
Pepper

Remove stalks and seeds from peppers; sauté them in oil and set aside. Sauté tomatoes in the remaining oil and cook for about 30 minutes over moderate heat or until a thick mass is formed. Beat eggs with cottage cheese, stir in garlic, parsley, salt and pepper. Add egg mixture to tomatoes and cook for 5 minutes over low heat. Serve this *fërgesë* as a garnish with the fried peppers. Serve hot.

4 servings.

POTATOES

Stuffed Potatoes
Patate të mbushura

a) *ground meat stuffing:*

2 pounds potatoes
1 cup chopped onions
1/4 cup oil
3/4 pound ground meat
1 tablespoon tomato sauce
Salt
Pepper
1 tablespoon chopped parsley
3 tablespoons shredded cheddar cheese

Preheat oven to 350°F.

Peel, wash and boil whole potatoes for a few minutes in salty water. Drain and cut each potato in half and remove the central part to make room for the stuffing. Sauté onion in oil until lightly brown. Add ground meat and sauté until browned. Add tomato sauce and 1/2 cup water, salt and pepper and cook until all liquid evaporates. Stir in parsley. Fill potatoes with meat mixture. Sprinkle with cheese and bake for 1/2 hour in a preheated oven at 350°F. Serve hot.

4 servings.

b) *eggs and cheese stuffing:*

2 pounds potatoes
3 eggs
1/2 cup shredded cheese
Pepper
1 tablespoon chopped parsley
2 tablespoons melted butter

Preheat oven to 350°F.

Prepare potatoes as in the above recipe. After the potato halves have been scooped, mash the scooped portion and mix it with eggs, cheese, pepper and parsley. Fill potatoes with this stuffing, sprinkle with melted butter and bake for 30 minutes in a preheated oven at 350°F.

4 servings.

Baked Potatoes
Patate të furrës

2 pounds potatoes
4 tablespoons oil
1 cup chopped onion
1 cup chopped, peeled tomatoes
1 cup chicken/beef gravy
Salt
Pepper
2 bay leaves

Peel, wash, slice and sauté potatoes lightly in oil. Remove them in a baking pan and sauté onion in the same oil until yellowish. Add tomatoes, gravy, salt, pepper and bay leaves and cook for 15 minutes. Mix with potatoes and bake for 30 minutes at 350°F or until all water evaporates.

Serve hot, as a main dish or to garnish other dishes.

4 servings.

Potato Musaka
Musaka me patate

2 pounds large potatoes
1/2 cup oil
1 cup chopped onions
1 pound ground meat
1 cup chopped, peeled tomatoes
Salt
Pepper
3 bay leaves
1 tablespoon chopped parsley
1 tablespoon bread crumbs
1 recipe bechamel sauce, p. 56
3 tablespoons shredded cheese

Peel, wash and cut potatoes into 1/4-inch thick slices and sauté in oil. Remove potatoes and sauté onion, then add meat and sauté until all moisture evaporates. Add tomatoes, salt, pepper, bay leaves, parsley, and a little water and cook for about 20 minutes or until meat is tender. Lay potato slices on a baking pan brushed with oil and sprinkled with bread crumbs, then alternate 2 layers of meat mixture and 2 layers of potato slices, with the last layer of potato slices on top. Prepare white (bechamel) sauce (see *Eggplant Mussaka*, p. 56, for the recipe). Cover potatoes with the sauce, sprinkle with cheese and bake for 1 hour at 375°F.

Serve hot.

4 servings.

Mashed Potatoes Rolls
Role pure patate

2 pounds potatoes
1/2 cup milk
2 raw eggs, divided
Salt
4 tablespoons butter, divided
2 onions, chopped
5 carrots, chopped
1 tablespoon chopped celery
4 tablespoons oil
Pepper
2 hard-boiled eggs
4 tablespoons bread crumbs
1 tablespoon chopped parsley

Wash and boil potatoes for about 15 minutes or until easily pierced with a fork. Peel potatoes and press through colander or food mill. Stir milk, 2 raw eggs, salt, and 2 tablespoons butter in with potatoes. Mix thoroughly, bring to a boil and cook for a few minutes until a thick purée is obtained. Sauté onions, carrots and celery in oil in a covered frying pan over low heat until tender. Season with salt and pepper and remove from heat. Dice 2 hard-boiled eggs and stir into the frying pan. Put a 3/4-inch layer of mashed potatoes on oilpaper, put a layer of onion mixture on top, and roll the oilpaper until both edges meet underneath. Remove the oilpaper, coat the potato roll-up with 2 beaten eggs, sprinkle with bread crumbs, parsley, and 2 tablespoons melted butter and bake for about 1 hour at 375°F or until a brownish crust is formed. Cut in serving pieces and serve hot.
4 servings.

Potato Croquettes
Qofte patatesh

2 pounds potatoes
4 eggs, divided
2 tablespoons butter
1/2 cup flour
1/4 cup shredded cheese
1 tablespoon chopped parsley
Salt
Pepper
Additional flour for coating
1/2 cup bread crumbs
3/4 cup oil

Peel and boil potatoes in hot salty water until tender. Purée boiled potatoes. Add 2 eggs, butter, flour, cheese, parsley, salt and pepper, and mix thoroughly until well blended. Shape potato mixture into 1-inch balls. Beat remaining eggs with a bit of water. Roll each potato ball in flour and beaten egg, and finally sprinkle with crumbs. Fry in hot oil. Serve hot.

4 servings.

SPINACH

Spinach Purée
Pure spinaqi

2 pounds spinach
2 tablespoons flour
5 tablespoons butter
1 cup milk
Salt
Pepper
3 eggs

Wash spinach and boil it in salty water for 5 minutes. Drain and purée the spinach, being careful to save some juice. Sauté flour lightly in butter, add milk, and mix continuously until a thick sauce is obtained. Add puréed spinach, season with salt and pepper, and bring to a boil. If too thick, add some spinach juice. Turn off heat and add eggs one at a time, mixing continuous-ly. Spinach purée may be served as a side dish or as a sauce/dip.
4 servings.

Spinach and Eggs
Spinaq me vezë

2 pounds spinach
1 bunch scallions, chopped
4 tablespoons butter
Salt
Pepper
Dill
4 eggs
1 cup hot milk

Wash spinach and boil it in salty water. Drain, squeeze and chop the spinach. Sauté scallions in butter, covered, until withered. Add spinach, salt, pepper and dill, mix thoroughly, and put mixture in a baking pan. Beat eggs and mix with hot milk. Pour egg mixture over spinach and bake for 20 minutes at 350°F. Serve immediately after removing from the oven, to preserve taste and appearance.
4 servings.

Spinach Croquettes
Qofte me spinaq

2 pounds spinach
4 tablespoons flour, divided
3 tablespoons butter
1 cup hot milk
3 eggs, divided
1/4 cup grated cheese
5 garlic cloves, minced
Salt
Pepper
1 teaspoon chopped parsley
Nutmeg
1/2 cup bread crumbs
3/4 cup oil

Boil spinach in salty water, drain, squeeze, and purée. Sauté 2 tablespoons flour lightly in butter, add hot milk, and stir continuously to avoid lumps. Add puréed spinach and cook for 5 minutes over low heat.

Remove from heat, cool a little, and stir in 2 eggs one at a time, mixing continuously. Add cheese and garlic, then season with salt, pepper, parsley and nutmeg.

When spinach mixture cools, shape into 1-inch croquettes. Roll successively in 1 beaten egg, 2 tablespoons flour, and bread crumbs. Fry croquettes in oil. Serve hot.

4 servings.

ZUCCHINI

Stuffed baked zucchini
Kunguj të mbushur të furrës

3 pounds medium-size zucchini
3/4 cup oil
2 large onions, minced
1/2 cup rice
1 pound ground meat
1/2 cup tomato juice, divided
Salt
Pepper
2 tablespoons chopped dill, divided
1/4 cup grated onion
2 tablespoons butter

Hollow out centers of zucchini, leaving shells no thicker than 1/4-inch. Sauté zucchini shells in hot oil and drain. Make stuffing by sautéeing together the chopped zucchini pulp and onions in the remaining oil. Add rice and ground meat and continue to sauté. Add 1/4 cup tomato juice, 1 cup water, salt, pepper and 1 tablespoon chopped dill, and cook over low heat until all moisture has cooked away. Fill zucchini shells with stuffing and lay them in a baking pan.

Prepare sauce: Sauté 1/4 cup grated onion in butter, add 1/4 cup tomato juice, 1/4 cup water, salt, pepper and remaining dill, and simmer for a couple of minutes. Cover zucchini with this sauce.

Bake for 20 minutes at 350°F. Serve hot.
4 servings.

Stuffed Zucchini in White Sauce
Kunguj të mbushur në salcë të bardhë

3 pounds zucchini
3/4 cup oil
2 large onions, minced
1/2 cup rice
1 pound ground meat
1/2 cup tomato juice, divided
Salt
Pepper
1 tablespoon chopped dill, divided
2 tablespoons flour
2 tablespoons butter
1 cup hot milk
1 cup beef stock
2 eggs
1/4 cup lemon juice

Prepare stuffed zucchini shells with the first 9 ingredients as in the Stuffed Zucchini recipe, p. 73. Put shells in a casserole with 2 cups salty water, cover with a heavy dish, and simmer for 10 minutes.

To make sauce: Sauté flour lightly in butter, and add hot milk, stirring continuously to avoid lumps. Add beef stock and boil for 8 minutes. Remove from heat, cool a little, and mix rapidly with small amounts of beaten eggs with lemon juice, one at a time, until a thin sauce is obtained. Cover zucchini with this sauce when serving, sprinkled with chopped dill.

4 servings.

Zucchini *Musaka*
Musaka me kunguj

3 pounds zucchini
3 tablespoons flour
3/4 cup oil
1 pound ground meat
1 cup finely grated onion
1 tablespoon tomato sauce
Salt
Pepper
3 tablespoons bread crumbs
1 recipe bechamel sauce (see p. 56)
2 tablespoons grated cheese
2 tablespoons melted butter

Cut zucchini lengthwise in 1/4-inch thick slices. Roll each slice in flour and sauté in oil. Remove zucchini and sauté meat and onion together. Add tomato sauce, salt and pepper, and a bit of water, and cook until most of the moisture has cooked away. Brush bottom of baking pan with oil, sprinkle with bread crumbs, and put layers of zucchini slices and meat mixture alternately, ending with zucchini slices on top. Prepare bechamel sauce (see *Eggplant Musaka*, p. 56, for the recipe), cover zucchini and meat mixture with it, sprinkle with cheese, and melted butter, and bake for 20 minutes at 350°F. Serve hot.

4 servings.

SOUPS
SUPAT

If you want excellent soup all you need is a stock rich in flavor and minerals, and a variety of vegetables. Save bones and meat scraps in the freezer, and also keep all vegetable leftovers. Delicious soup stock can be made by simmering chopped bones and meat scraps for about 30 minutes in the pressure cooker. You may add some vinegar to help dissolve calcium, as well as salt while boiling.

Vegetables used in making soup stock should be cooked only a short time, in order to retain their flavor and vitamin C content. When vegetables are thoroughly chopped and quickly cooked in soup stock, most of the various vitamins contained in them pass into the stock. If you boil vegetables slowly for 15 minutes, the greater part of their minerals is also extracted into the stock. You will consequently obtain a stock very rich in vitamins and minerals. Before using it to prepare your soup, you should strain it through a cloth to remove bone splinters. You can also use the cloth to squeeze all the juices from the boiled vegetables.

Soup stock may be used in preparing a lot of other dishes. You can improve taste considerably by adding soup stock instead when a recipe calls for water. Cream-based soups become creamier, more delicious, and more nutritious by adding some powdered milk.

Vegetable Soup
Supë perimesh

1 onion, grated
1/4 cup olive oil, butter or margarine
2 carrots
1/4 pound green beans
1/4 pound peas
1 tablespoon tomato sauce, or 1/2 cup chopped tomatoes
5 cups meat stock
1 tablespoon flour
1 pound potatoes, peeled and cubed
Salt
Pepper
2 tablespoons chopped parsley

Sauté onion in oil until tender. Peel, wash and cut carrots in 1/2-inch squares, and cut green beans in halves. Sauté carrots, beans, and peas with the onion for a few minutes. Add tomato sauce and meat stock and boil over low heat for 8 minutes. Add flour and mix thoroughly. Add potatoes and boil for another 15 minutes. Season with salt, pepper and parsley. Serve hot.
4 servings.

Entrails Soup
Supë magjericë

1 bunch green onions, chopped
3 tablespoons butter
1/2 pound lamb or mutton entrails
1/4 cup rice
2 eggs
2 tablespoons lemon juice
Salt
Pepper
Parsley
Dill

Sauté onions in butter until tender. Dip entrails in 3 cups boiling water for 1 minute, drain and slice in small squares. Sauté entrails with the onion, add 4 cups water, bring to a boil and add rice. Cook until rice is tender. Remove from heat and cool for 10 minutes. Stir in small portions of beaten eggs with lemon juice, and season with salt, pepper, parsley and dill. Serve hot.

4 servings.

Potato Soup
Supë patatesh

1 onion, finely grated
3 tablespoons butter or margarine
1 pound potatoes, peeled and sliced
1/2 pound tomatoes, peeled and chopped
5 cups meat stock
Salt
Pepper
Parsley

Sauté onion in butter until tender. Add sliced potatoes and continue to sauté. Add tomatoes and sauté. Stir in meat stock and cook for 20 minutes. Season with salt, pepper and parsley. Serve hot.

4 servings.

Potato and Cabbage Soup
Supë borsh me patate e lakër

1 onion, grated
3 tablespoons oil or margarine
2 carrots, finely chopped
3 celery stalks, finely chopped
1 tablespoon flour
1 tablespoon tomato sauce
5 cups meat stock
1 pound cabbage, finely chopped
2 tablespoons vinegar
1 pound potatoes, diced
2 beet roots, diced
Salt
Pepper
4 tablespoons cream

Sauté onion lightly in oil. Add carrots and celery and continue to sauté. Add flour and sauté. Add tomato sauce and a few tablespoons stock slowly, stirring continuously. Cook over low heat until the sauce is ready. Boil the remaining stock and add cabbage. Add vinegar and cook for 15 minutes, then add potatoes and beet roots and cook for 20 minutes over low heat. Stir in the sauce and cook for another 5 minutes. Season with salt and pepper and serve hot, covered with a tablespoon of cream for each dish.
4 servings.

Rice Soup
Supë orizi

5 cups meat stock
1/4 cup rice
3 tablespoons butter or margarine
2 eggs
2 tablespoons lemon juice
Salt
Pepper
Parsley

Bring stock to a boil, add rice and butter and cook over low heat for 30 minutes. Remove from heat, let cool for 10 minutes and mix slowly with small portions of beaten eggs with lemon juice. Season with salt, pepper and parsley. Serve hot.
    4 servings.

Mutton Breast Soup
Çorbë me gjoks dashi

1 pound mutton breast
1/4 cup rice
1 onion, finely grated
3 tomatoes, peeled and finely grated
2 tablespoons butter
6 garlic cloves, finely grated
1 teaspoon chili powder
Salt
2 tablespoons chopped parsley

Slice mutton in 1/2-inch squares and cook over low heat for 45 minutes in 5 cups salty water. Add rice and onion and cook for another 30 minutes. Sauté tomatoes in butter, remove from heat, and add garlic and hot pepper. Add small amounts of the mutton stock, stirring thoroughly until a sauce is obtained. Add salt to taste. Mix this sauce with the stock and bring to a boil. Serve hot, seasoned with parsley.

4 servings.

Fish Soup
Supë peshku

1 pound fish
2 tablespoons vinegar
1 onion, finely grated
1/4 cup olive oil
3 carrots, chopped
1 celery stalk, chopped
1 tablespoon flour
1/2 pound tomatoes, peeled and chopped
1 pound potatoes, peeled and sliced
2 garlic cloves, finely grated
Salt
Pepper
Parsley
Oregano

Boil fish slowly in 5 cups boiling water and vinegar for 5 minutes. Remove fish and slice it. Reserve stock. Sauté onion in olive oil until tender, then add carrots and celery and sauté. Add flour and tomatoes, and sauté for a couple of minutes. Stir in fish stock, and cook over low heat for 5 minutes. Add potatoes, fish slices, garlic, salt, pepper, parsley, and oregano and cook for 30 minutes. Serve hot.

4 servings.

Chicken and Noodles Soup
Supë pule me makarona peta

2 eggs
1/4 cup milk
Salt
1 1/2 cups flour
1 1/2 pounds chicken
1 onion, chopped
2 carrots, chopped
3 tablespoons butter
Pepper
Parsley

Make noodles:

Combine eggs, milk, 1 teaspoon salt, flour and enough water to make a stiff dough. Knead well and roll 1/16 inch thick, let dry 20 minutes and cut into strips 1/4 inch wide. Cut strips into 2-inch long pieces and let dry.

Stew chicken in 6 cups water. Remove chicken meat from bones, slice it, and return meat to the stock. Sauté onion and carrots in butter and add to the chicken stock. Bring stock to a boil, add salt and drop in noodles so slowly that boiling does not stop. Reduce heat, add salt, pepper, and parsley and simmer, covered, for 15 minutes. Serve hot.

4 servings.

Ground Beef Soup
Çorbë shkodrane

1/2 cup grated onion
3 tablespoons butter
1/2 pound ground beef
1 tablespoon tomato sauce
1/2 cup rice
5 cups meat stock
Salt
Pepper
Parsley

Sauté onion lightly in butter. Add meat and continue to sauté. Add tomato sauce, rice and meat stock, and cook for 30 minutes over low heat. Season with salt, pepper, and parsley. Serve hot.
4 servings.

Lamb Entrails Soup
Çorbë me të brendshme qingji

1 pound lamb entrails
1/4 cup rice
2 teaspoons flour
5 tablespoons butter
1 cup yogurt
6 garlic cloves, finely grated
Salt
Pepper

Cook lamb entrails in 4 cups water until tender. Drain and dice entrails, reserving stock. Return entrails to the stock and bring to a boil. Add rice and cook for another 20 minutes. Sauté flour in butter, remove from heat, mix thoroughly with cold water, and stir into the soup. Mix yogurt with garlic, salt, and pepper, and stir into the soup. Serve hot.
4 servings.

Yogurt Broth
Paçe me kos

1 cup flour
1/2 cup olive oil
4 cups meat stock
6 garlic cloves, finely grated
Salt
3 tablespoons vinegar
1 cup yogurt
Pepper

Sauté flour in oil until brown. Add stock, mix thoroughly, and bring to a boil. Crush garlic with salt, mix with vinegar and yogurt, and stir this mixture into the boiling stock. Season with pepper to taste. Serve hot.
4 servings.

Head Broth
Paçe koke

2 pounds lamb, mutton, or veal head
3 carrots, finely grated
1 onion, finely grated
Celery seed
Salt
1 tablespoon flour
2 tablespoons butter
1 teaspoon tomato sauce
Pepper
Mild red pepper
6 garlic cloves
1/4 cup vinegar

Clean, wash, and cut head in pieces. Place pieces in cold water to remove blood. Put pieces in a stock pot with 6 cups cold water, bring to a boil, and skim. Cook broth over low heat with carrots, onion, celery seed, and salt until meat is tender. Remove meat from the bones and slice it. Pass stock through a colander, and mix stock with meat slices.

Sauté flour in butter until brown, add tomato sauce and mix with a bit of stock until a sauce is formed. Stir the sauce into the meat stock, add pepper and red pepper, and cook over low heat for 20 minutes. Add garlic and vinegar. Serve hot.

4 servings.

Tripe Broth and Tomato Sauce
Paçe plëndësi me salcë domatesh

2 pounds tripe
3 tablespoons vinegar
1 tablespoon tomato sauce
1 tablespoon flour
1/4 cup oil
Chili powder
Salt
8 garlic cloves, finely grated

Clean tripe thoroughly, combine with 6 cups cold water and vinegar, and bring to a boil. Skim and cook over low heat until tender (about 3 hours in a covered casserole or 1 hour in a pressure cooker). Remove tripe, slice in 1-inch squares and return to the stock.

Sauté tomato sauce and flour in oil, add chili powder and a bit of tripe stock, and cook for 15 minutes. Add salt and garlic, and stir the mixture into the tripe stock. Serve hot.

4 servings.

Tripe Broth and Eggs
Paçe plëndësi me vezë e limon

2 pounds tripe
1/2 cup oil
1 tablespoon flour
2 eggs
2 tablespoons lemon juice
Salt
Pepper

Clean tripe thoroughly, put in a stock pot with 6 cups cold water, and bring to a boil. Skim and cook over low heat until tender. Remove tripe (reserving stock), slice in 1-inch squares, and sauté lightly in oil. Add flour and sauté until yellow. Return tripe to the stock, bring to a boil, and remove from heat. Cool stock and then stir in eggs beaten with lemon juice, salt, and pepper. Serve hot.
4 servings.

CLEAR STOCK SOUPS
SUPAT E KTHJELLËTA

To prepare a stock of meat and bones: boil meat and bones in a pot until meat is tender; put chopped vegetable parings into a cloth bag, and then put the bag in the pot and boil for 10 minutes. Squeeze juices from parings and discard bones, returning meat to soup. To clear stock, reheat strained stock and add several egg shells or the uncooked white of one egg. Stir thoroughly, simmer 5 minutes, and strain.

Clear Stock and Puffs Soup
Supë e kthjellët me qofte

1 pound ground meat
2 eggs, divided
1/4 cup finely grated onion
2 tablespoons ground parsley
1 garlic clove, minced
1/2 cup powdered milk
1/2 cup tomato juice
Salt
Pepper
1 tablespoon powdered milk
1/2 cup bread crumbs
2 tablespoons butter
5 cups clear stock

Combine ground beef, 1 egg plus 1 egg white, onion, parsley, garlic, 1/2 cup powdered milk, tomato juice, salt, and pepper, and knead well. Press into 1-inch balls, roll in egg yolk beaten with 1 tablespoon powdered milk, and then roll in bread crumbs. Brown meatballs in hot butter over medium-high heat for 8 minutes. Put meatballs and stock in a pan and cook in the oven at 300°F for 30 minutes. Serve hot.
4 servings.

Clear Stock and Vegetables Soup
Supë e kthjellët me perime

2 pounds various vegetables (carrots, onion, celery, spinach,
    peas, green beans, etc.)
5 cups clear stock
2 tablespoons butter
1 garlic clove, finely grated
Salt
Pepper
2 tablespoons chopped parsley

Chop spinach and dip in boiling stock for 1 minute. Boil peas and green beans for 6 minutes in boiling stock. Dice onion, carrots, and celery stalks and sauté lightly in butter. Boil sautéed vegetables in stock for 10 minutes. Mix all vegetables. Add garlic, salt and pepper to taste to the stock. Serve vegetables in separate dishes, covering them with stock. Garnish with parsley.
4 servings.

Clear Stock and Noodles Soup
Supë e kthjellët me makarona

1 pound noodles
Salt
5 cups clear stock

Boil noodles for 5 minutes in boiling salted water, drain and rinse in hot water. Put noodles in a bowl, then cover with hot stock. Serve hot.
4 servings.

CREAM SOUPS
SUPAT KREM

Cream soups are easy to make and excellent as a first course for dinner. Powdered milk should be added to cream soups in order to improve nutritive value and taste. These soups should not be boiled. To make cream soups you can use all kinds of vegetables, poultry, veal, entrails, etc.

Cream Soup and Meatballs
Supë krem me qofte

1 pound ground meat
1/2 cup finely grated onion
3 tablespoons chopped parsley
2 eggs, separated
1 tablespoon rice (half-boiled)
Salt
Pepper
5 cups meat stock
2 tablespoons lemon juice
2 tablespoons flour
4 tablespoons butter or margarine
1 1/2 cups milk

Mix thoroughly and knead well: meat, onion, parsley, egg whites, half-boiled rice, salt and pepper. Make into 1-inch balls and put them in a casserole with boiling stock and lemon juice for 15 minutes.

Sauté flour in butter until yellow, then stir in small quantities of milk and stock until a liquid sauce is obtained. Add the remaining milk and stock, stir in egg yolks beaten with a bit of soup, then put meatballs and parsley into the soup.

Serve hot.

4 servings.

Cream of Chicken Soup
Supë krem pule

1/2 cup finely grated carrots
1/2 cup finely grated onion
1 green pepper, finely grated
3 cups chicken stock
1 cup milk
Salt
Pepper
2 tablespoons flour
3 tablespoons butter
2 egg yolks
1 cup diced chicken

Add carrots, onion and grated pepper to stock and cook for 10 minutes. Add milk and simmer for another 10 minutes. Season with salt and pepper to taste.

Sauté flour slightly in hot butter, add bits of milk and stock stirring continuously until a sauce is obtained. Mix this sauce with the stock, bring to a boil, remove from heat and mix thoroughly with the egg yolks. Add chicken cubes, mix, and serve hot.

4 servings.

Creamy Potato Soup
Supë krem patatesh

1 pound potatoes, finely diced
5 cups meat stock
1 onion, finely grated
2 carrots, chopped fine
2 tablespoons chopped parsley
4 tablespoons butter, divided
1/4 cup bechamel sauce (see *Eggplant Musaka*, p. 56 for recipe)
2 egg yolks
1 cup hot milk
2 slices bread, cubed
Salt

Peel, dice and simmer potatoes for 5 minutes in hot meat stock. Sauté onion, carrots, and parsley in 2 tablespoons butter. Add sautéed vegetables to stock and simmer, covered, for 10 minutes. Drain, crush and strain the vegetables. Add a bit of liquid, beat until smooth and mix thoroughly with bechamel sauce. Bring to a boil, let cool then mix with yolks beaten with hot milk. Use remaining butter to sauté diced bread and serve soup with sautéed bread cubes on top. Season with salt to taste.
4 servings.

Mixed Vegetables Cream Soup
Supë krem perimesh

2 cups chopped or grated vegetables (spinach, carrots,
    onion, beans, peas, celery, parsley, peppers, potatoes)
3 tablespoons butter, divided
4 cups meat stock
1 cup powdered milk
2 tablespoons bechamel sauce (see *Eggplant Musaka*, p. 56)
Salt
1 egg yolk

Sauté onion, carrots and celery in 2 tablespoons butter. Simmer other vegetables, covered, in hot stock for 10 minutes. Add sautéed vegetables and simmer for another 5 minutes. Stir in powdered milk and bechamel sauce, season with salt, and bring to a boil. Remove from heat. Cool and mix with the beaten egg yolk. Put the remaining butter on top, and serve hot, with toast.

4 servings.

Spinach Cream Soup
Supë krem spinaqi

1/2 cup finely grated onion
3/4 cup finely grated carrots
4 tablespoons butter, divided
3 pounds spinach
5 cups meat stock
1 recipe bechamel sauce, p. 56
1/2 cup bread crumbs
Salt

Sauté onion and carrots lightly in 2 tablespoons butter. Add sautéed vegetables, with spinach, to boiling stock for 10 minutes, then strain. Prepare bechamel sauce (see *Eggplant Musaka*, p. 56), stir in the soup and cook for another 3 minutes over low heat. Serve hot, smothered with remaining butter and crumbs. Season with salt to taste.

4 servings.

TRAHANA
TRAHANA

There are various kinds of *trahana*, depending on the ingredients used to prepare them. Basically *trahana* is a leavened dough, dried and made into crumbs, which are then used to prepare a bread soup. The most popular *trahanas* are those prepared with yogurt, milk, tomato juice, and bouillon, respectively. Trahana dough must be made of sifted hard-wheat, a high-protein flour rich in gluten.

To prepare trahana crumbs:

a) *yogurt trahana*: 1 package/cake crumbled baker's yeast
7 cups all-purpose flour
2 cups yogurt
4 tablespoons melted butter
1 teaspoon salt

Stir yeast in 1/2 cup warm water, then combine it with the other ingredients. Stir well, but don't knead. Cover bowl and set in a warm place at 90°F. Let rise until double in bulk and spread over a clean cloth. Let dry, crumble, sift, then crumble again.

Keep in a cloth bag, not in a plastic one, and preserve in a cool and dry place.

b) *milk trahana*:

> 1 package/cake crumbled baker's yeast
> 7 cups all-purpose flour
> 2 cups milk
> 4 tablespoons butter
> 1 teaspoon salt

c) *tomato juice trahana*:

> 1 package/cake crumbled baker's yeast
> 7 cups all-purpose flour
> 2 cups tomato juice
> 4 tablespoons butter
> 1 teaspoon salt

d) *bouillon trahana*:

> 1 package/cake crumbled baker's yeast
> 7 cups all-purpose flour
> 2 cups bouillon
> 2 tablespoons butter
> 1 teaspoon salt

Follow the same procedure as in the basic recipe above (*yogurt trahana*) to prepare the dough and the trahana crumbs.

Trahana Soup
Trahana me bukë të thekur

1 cup trahana crumbs
4 cups diced toast
3/4 cup finely diced feta cheese
4 tablespoons butter
Red pepper powder
4 tablespoons olive oil

Put trahana crumbs in a bowl, stir in 2 cups cold water and let crumbs soak for 2 hours. Stir the crumbs in the bowl. Put 2 cups hot water in a casserole, bring to a boil, then stir in the soaked crumbs. Simmer for 5 minutes, stirring continuously, then remove trahana soup from heat. Put diced toast in four bowls or deep dishes, and stir in trahana soup. Spoon diced feta cheese over each bowl. Melt butter in a saucepan, add mild red pepper, sauté 1 minute, then spoon butter over the bowls. Sprinkle with olive oil. Serve immediately.
4 servings.

FISH
PESHQIT

Fish can be served not only in place of meat but in addition to it. Fish contains approximately the same amount of protein as does meat, little fat, and can do much to overcome protein deficiencies. It is rich in phosphorus; sea fish are excellent sources of iodine.

It is important to know that the flavor and deliciousness of any fish are in proportion to the amount of juices retained during cooking. Since salt draws out juices, flavor and nutritive value, fish should be salted only when it is served. Fish may be salted before being cooked when it is rolled in flour or crumbs or dipped in batter which catches juices so they are drawn out. The cooking time for fish should be short. Generally, fish is considered to be perfectly cooked when no juices are lost and yet all proteins are well cooked. Thus, fish should be taken up when the internal temperature reaches about 150°F. In addition to that, there is no odor when you cook fish at temperatures under 150°F.

Fish should never be boiled. At that temperature flavor and nutritive value soak out, and most juices are lost. Also, it should not be overcooked, or browned while roasting or broiling. A golden color may be attained without overcooking. A brown color can be easily obtained by sprinkling the fish with paprika before cooking. Also, frozen fish should be thawed at room temperature and cooked immediately. In Albanian cooking most fish are fried or baked. In general, large fish are usually baked, whereas fillets and steaks are broiled or sautéed and served with sauce.

There is not as much need to suggest specific types of fish with each recipe as the size and type of cut. Anyway, certain traditional Albanian fish dishes require certain varieties of fish found in the Mediterranean, like bass, mullet, red mullet, flounder, cod, eel, etc.

Baked Fish and Onions
Tavë peshku

2 pounds whole fish
1/2 cup oil
1 1/2 pounds onions
12 garlic cloves
1/2 pound tomatoes, peeled and chopped
1/4 cup vinegar
2 tablespoons chopped parsley
Salt
Pepper
3 bay leaves

Cut fish into 1-inch thick steaks and sauté in part of the oil until brownish. Cut onions in thin half-circle slices and sauté together with garlic cloves under cover until tender. Add tomatoes, sauté lightly, add vinegar, parsley, salt, pepper and bay leaves, bring to a boil, then put in a baking pan with the fish steaks seasoned with salt and pepper on top. Bake at 300°F for about 45 minutes. Serve hot.

4 servings.

Fried Fish
Peshk i skuqur

2 pounds small whole fish
Salt
4 tablespoons flour
2 eggs
2 lemons (use for rind and slices)
1/2 cup bread crumbs
1 cup oil
Pepper
Parsley

Clean fish, season with salt and let drain. Dredge in a mixture of flour, eggs, grated lemon rind and 1 teaspoon salt, then dredge in bread crumbs. Heat oil until very hot and lay fish in the frying pan. Do not cover the frying pan. Turn as soon as golden, or in about 5 minutes, and let another 3 minutes. Take up immediately after both sides are browned. Season with pepper and garnish with parsley. Serve with lemon slices around, accompanied with salad.
    4 servings.

Bass in White Sauce
Lavrak në salcë të bardhë

1 pound potatoes
3 carrots
3 onions
1 cup vinegar
6 garlic cloves
2 bay leaves
Salt
Oregano
3 tablespoons chopped parsley
Pepper
3 pounds large bass, cleaned and cut into pieces

For the *white sauce:*

4 tablespoons flour
4 tablespoons butter
4 cups fish bouillon

Cut peeled potatoes, carrots and onions coarsely, put in a stock pot together with vinegar, garlic cloves, bay leaves, salt, oregano, parsley and pepper to taste. Add 4 cups hot water, bring to a boil, and simmer for 30 minutes. Remove boiled vegetables from the casserole and let drain. Put fish pieces in the pot and simmer for 20 minutes.

Sauté flour lightly in butter, then gradually add 4 cups of fish bouillon mixing continuously over low heat until blended and slightly thickened. Serve fish surrounded with boiled vegetables and this sauce.

4 servings.

Baked Fish and Potatoes
Tavë peshku me patate

3 pounds whole fish (bass, carp, mullet, trout, tuna, etc.)
Salt
Pepper
Oregano
1 cup olive oil, divided
5 garlic cloves, finely grated
Parsley
2 pounds potatoes, sliced
3 tablespoons lemon juice
1 cup white wine

Clean, wash and drain fish, and season with salt, pepper and oregano. Put half of the oil, garlic and parsley in a baking pan, season with salt, mix thoroughly and spread the mixture to cover the bottom. Set fish with its back up, put potatoes around and bake at 300°F for 25–30 minutes, sprinkling occasionally with a mixture of lemon juice, white wine and 1/4 cup oil. Serve promptly.

4 servings.

Poached Red Mullet
Tavë me barbun

2 pounds small red mullets
1 tablespoon flour
1/2 cup oil
Salt
Pepper
1 pound peeled tomatoes, finely sliced
2 tablespoons lemon juice
Parsley
1 pound onions, finely sliced

Dredge red mullets in flour and sauté lightly in hot oil until yellowish and still only partially done. Season with salt and pepper and place in a baking dish sprinkled with oil. Sauté onion lightly in filtered remaining oil under cover without stirring, then add tomatoes, season, and let cook under cover over low heat for 20 minutes, just shaking the frying pan occasionally. Add 2 cups hot water and simmer for another 20 minutes until a thick sauce is obtained. Smother red mullets with this sauce and bake at 350°F for 15 minutes, occasionally basting with the sauce and sprinkling with lemon juice. Sprinkle with parsley and serve immediately.

4 servings.

Broiled Mullet
Qefull i skarës

2 pounds (5–6 whole) mullets
1/4 cup oil
Dry mustard
2 tablespoons lemon juice
Paprika
Salt
6 garlic cloves, finely grated
Red pepper powder
4 tablespoons butter
Lemon slices
2 tablespoons chopped parsley

Brush fish with oil outside and with mustard inside, then sprinkle generously with lemon juice and paprika, and set aside for 10 minutes. Set broiler pan so that fish is about 1 inch from the very small flames, or about 4 inches from heating unit if using electricity. Place fish on broiler pan. Turn fish after 10 minutes and remove from heat after another 8 minutes. Season with salt. Mix garlic, pepper and salt with butter, and smother fish with this mixture while serving. Garnish with lemon slices and parsley.
4 servings.

Baked Trout with Walnuts
Troftë tavë me arra

1 whole trout (2–3 pounds)
Salt
Pepper
2 tablespoons flour
4 tablespoons oil
15 peeled, crushed walnuts
Dill
1 lemon (for rind and slices)

Preheat oven to 350°F.

Clean the fish, remove organs and slice across the grain without skinning or removing bones. Season steaks with salt and pepper, dredge in flour and sauté lightly in oil. Remove steaks and put them in a baking pan. Sauté the remaining flour in the remaining oil until brownish, add 1 cup hot water and walnuts, mix well and bring to a boil. Season with salt, pepper and dill, spoon this sauce over the fish, sprinkle with grated lemon rind, and bake for 20 minutes. Sprinkle with grated walnuts and serve immediately, garnished with lemon sections.

4 servings.

Stuffed Trout
Trofta të mbushura

2 pounds (4 whole) trout
1/2 cup chopped onion
1/2 cup oil
1 cup crumbled feta cheese
1 cup bread crumbs
3 tablespoons chopped parsley
Dill
Salt
Pepper
1 lemon, sliced
2 carrots, sliced

Preheat oven to 300°F.

Clean fish, cut the head off and remove organs without cutting the abdomen. Take the ribs and the backbone out by cutting fish in half along the backbone from the outside and loosening flesh from bones by pushing it back with the dull edge of a knife. Sauté onion in 1/4 cup oil and mix it thoroughly with cheese, crumbs, parsley, dill, salt and pepper. Stuff fish with this dressing, sew their backs, brush with the remaining oil and bake at 300°F. Allow approximately 30 minutes for heat to penetrate about 2 inches. Garnish with lemon slices, steamed carrots and pickles.

4 servings.

Cod in White Wine
Merluc me verë të bardhë

1 pound onions, finely sliced
1/2 cup oil
1 cup white wine
1 tablespoon tomato sauce
Salt
Pepper
Dill
2 pounds large cod
3 tablespoons lemon juice
2 tablespoons chopped parsley

Sauté onions lightly in oil. Add wine, tomato sauce, salt, pepper and dill to taste, then cook for 20 minutes over low heat. Skin fish, slice, wash, drain and sprinkle with lemon juice and salt. Drain again after 10 minutes and lay the fish slices in a pan, then smother with the sauce. Cook over low heat for 30 minutes and serve cold, sprinkled with parsley.
4 servings.

Baked Bass and Feta Cheese
Tavë lavraku me djathë

4 tablespoons butter
1 cup crumbed feta cheese
1/2 cup chopped onion
1 cup milk
1 teaspoon dry mustard
Salt
Pepper
3 pounds bass

Brush the baking pan with butter and put half the cheese, onion and butter in it. Bring milk to a boil, put it in a bowl together with half the cheese, 1 teaspoon mustard, salt and pepper; mix thoroughly in order to obtain a uniform mass, and spoon this mixture over the fish. Bake for 30 minutes at 350°F. Serve hot, accompanied with salad.

4 servings.

Marinated Fish
Peshk marinadë

2 pounds small—4 to 5 inches long—fish: (mullet, red mullet, bass, trout, cod, etc.)
4 tablespoons lemon juice, divided
Salt
Pepper
3/4 cup oil
6 garlic cloves, finely grated
2 tablespoons flour
1/2 cup red wine vinegar
1/2 teaspoon sugar
1 1/2 cups tomato juice
Rosemary
Basil
1/4 cup olive oil

Wash, drain and sprinkle fish with 2 tablespoons lemon juice. Season with salt and pepper and let marinate for 1 hour. Sauté fish lightly in hot oil and let cool in a large deep dish. Sauté garlic in the remaining oil until yellowish, add flour and sauté until brownish. Stir in 1 cup water, remaining lemon juice, vinegar, sugar, and tomato sauce, and cook over low heat stirring continously until well blended and slightly thickened. Adjust seasoning with salt, pepper, rosemary and basil. Spoon this sauce over the fish, sprinkle with olive oil. Chill and serve cold garnished with lemon slices.

4 servings.

Browned Fish Fillets
Peshk filetë i fërguar

2 pounds fish (1/2 pound each)
2 tablespoons lemon juice
1/4 cup olive oil
2 tablespoons chopped parsley
Salt
Pepper
4 tablespoons sifted whole-wheat-bread crumbs
2 eggs, beaten
3/4 cup oil
Garnish: lemon slices, cabbage pickles, olives, parsley sprigs

Put fish in a large bowl and marinate in a mixture of lemon juice, olive oil, parsley, salt and pepper. Dredge fillets in bread crumbs, then in beaten eggs, and lay them in hot oil (not above 150°F). Turn as soon as golden, or in about 4 minutes, and brown the other side, without covering utensil. Take up after well browned on both sides.

Serve immediately, garnished with lemon slices, cabbage pickles, large olives and parsley sprigs.

4 servings.

Baked Trout, Potatoes and Tomatoes
Troftë tavë me patate e domate

2 tablespoons finely grated garlic
2 tablespoons chopped parsley
1/2 cup bread crumbs, divided
1/4 cup tomato juice
1 cup white wine
1 cup oil
1/4 cup lemon juice
Salt
Pepper
2 pounds trout
1 pound tomatoes, steamed, peeled and sliced
1 pound potatoes, boiled, peeled and sliced
2 tablespoons olive oil

Mix garlic, parsley and 1/4 cup crumbs together, and use part of the mixture to dot the oil-coated bottom of the baking pan. Mix well tomato juice, wine, oil, 1/4 cup lemon juice, and season with salt and pepper. Lay fish on the baking pan, cover with tomato slices and baste with this mixture, then sprinkle with the remaining crumbs. Bake at 300°F for 30 minutes. Serve hot, accompanied with potato slices sprinkled with olive oil, lemon juice and salt.

4 servings.

Baked Mullet and Oranges
Qefull tavë me portokaj

1/4 cup tomato juice
2 tablespoons lemon juice
1 cup olive oil
1 cup white wine
5 garlic cloves, finely grated
Salt
Pepper
1/2 cup bread crumbs
3 tablespoons chopped parsley, divided
2 pounds large whole mullet
2 oranges, sliced
2 tomatoes, sliced
1/2 pound potatoes, boiled, peeled and sliced
Dill

Mix well tomato juice, lemon juice, oil, wine, garlic, salt and pepper to taste, and spread 3/4 of the mixture onto the bottom of a baking pan. Mix bread crumbs with 2 tablespoons parsley and spoon 3/4 of this mixture over the first one. Wash, drain and salt the fish, then lay it on top. Cover fish with orange and tomato slices and smother in turn with what has remained of the first and the second mixture. Bake at 350°F until well done on both sides, or for about 30 minutes, continuously basting with the drippings.

Serve hot, garnished with boiled potatoes seasoned with salt, parsley, lemon juice, dill, and a bit of olive oil.

4 servings.

Seasoned Broiled Cod Fillets
Merluc fileto i skarës

2 pounds cod fillets
1/4 cup lemon juice
2 tablespoons chopped parsley
1/4 cup oil
Salt
Pepper
1/2 cup sifted bread crumbs
1 egg beaten
4 tablespoons butter

Marinate fillets for 15 minutes in a mixture of lemon juice, parsley, oil, salt and pepper. Drain, dredge first in bread crumbs then in the beaten egg, sauté lightly in butter and broil at 350°F for about 15 minutes. Serve with French-fried potatoes and mayonnaise.
4 servings.

Flounder Fillets and Spinach Soufflé
Fileto shojze me sufle spinaqi

2 pounds flounder fillets
4 tablespoons melted butter
1 cup white wine
5 garlic cloves, finely grated
2 bay leaves
Salt
Pepper
2 pounds spinach, chopped
3 eggs, separated
2 tablespoons chopped parsley
Dried celery
1/4 cup lemon juice
2–3 tablespoons oil

Wash and drain fillets, and lay them onto the bottom of the baking pan brushed with melted butter, add wine, garlic and bay leaves and sprinkle with salt and pepper. Cover the pan with oilpaper and bake at 300°F for 25 minutes, basting occasionally with the sauce.

Meanwhile simmer spinach 5 minutes, stirring occasionally. Remove from heat, cool slightly, then add 3 egg yolks, chopped parsley, a bit of dried celery, salt and pepper to taste, and lemon juice; stir well.

Beat and fold in 3 egg whites, pour into casserole brushed with oil and put in a preheated oven at 300°F. Bake for 45 minutes. Serve fillets garnished with spinach soufflé.

4 servings.

Baked Sardines
Sardele të furrës

2 pounds headless sardines
1/2 cup olive oil
Salt
Pepper
Oregano
1/4 cup lemon juice
6 bay leaves
1 tablespoon fresh chopped dill

Wash, drain and lay as many fish as will easily fit onto the bottom of a baking pan, brushed with oil. Sprinkle with salt, pepper, oregano, dill, lemon juice and oil, spread the bay leaves over fish, then put another layer of sardines on top. Sprinkle again with the above ingredients, then bake at 350°F for about 25 minutes. Serve hot or cold, with mayonnaise or various salads. Garnish with the chopped dill.

4 servings.

Stuffed Squids
Kallamarë të mbushur

4 whole squids
3/4 cup chopped onion
1/2 cup oil
3/4 cup rice
4 tomatoes, peeled and chopped
2 tablespoons chopped parsley
Celery powder
Salt
Pepper

Wash and drain squids, cut off tentacles and cut them in small pieces. Sauté onion in oil lightly, add rice and sauté. Add tentacle pieces, tomatoes, a bit of water, parsley, celery powder, salt and pepper. When rice is half-boiled remove from heat and stuff squids with this mixture. Put them in a baking pan, add 1 cup hot water and bake at 350°F for half an hour. Serve hot.

4 servings.

Cuttle-fish and Rice
Sepje me oriz

2 pounds cuttle-fish
2 cups brown rice
4 tablespoons butter
Salt
Pepper
1/2 cup diced cheese
2 tablespoons chopped parsley

Wash and drain cuttle-fish, then remove everything inside them. Cut fish in small pieces and boil in 4 cups water until tender.

Place rice in a wire strainer and wash quickly under running water. Shake dry and fry in butter, stirring continously, until well browned. Add 3 cups hot water, butter, salt, pepper and cook over low heat for about 45 minutes, or until tender. Just before serving add cuttle-fish, cheese and parsley. Stir well and serve immediately, accompanied with green salad.

4 servings.

Fish Croquettes
Qofte peshku

2 eggs, separated
3 cups leftover fish, or 1 1/2 pounds fresh fish fillets, diced
4 tablespoons flour
1/4 cup powdered milk
1 finely chopped onion
1 teaspoon minced garlic
3 tablespoons chopped parsley
Salt
Pepper
Oregano
1/2 cup bread crumbs
1 cup oil

Beat egg yolks in a bowl, add fish, flour, milk, onion, garlic, parsley, salt, pepper and oregano and mix well. Beat egg whites stiff and add to the mixture, stirring continuously. Make into patties, roll in crumbs, and sauté in oil.

Serve hot, with salad or bechamel sauce (see p. 56).

4 servings.

Shrimp Salad
Sallatë me karkaleca deti

1 1/2 pounds shrimp, shelled and cleaned
3/4 cup sliced carrots
1/2 cup sliced onions
2 bay leaves
1 tablespoon grated garlic
1/4 cup vinegar
3 tablespoons chopped parsley
Oregano
Salt
Pepper
1/4 cup lemon juice
1/2 cup olive oil

Wash and drain shrimps. Put carrots, onions, bay leaves, garlic, vinegar, parsley, oregano, salt and pepper in a stock pot and bring to a boil. Add shrimps and cook for 10 minutes over low heat, under cover. Remove shrimps, let them cool down, and sprinkle with lemon juice and olive oil. Serve with mayonnaise.
4 servings.

Shrimp in White Wine
Karkaleca me verë të bardhë

1/2 cup chopped onions
1/4 cup oil
1 cup peeled, chopped tomatoes
1/4 cup grated carrots
1 cup white wine
1 garlic clove, finely grated
Salt
Pepper
2 pounds shrimp, shelled and cleaned
2 tablespoons olive oil
2 tablespoons chopped parsley

Sauté onions in oil, add tomatoes and carrots, and sauté for 3 minutes; stir in wine, garlic, salt and pepper to taste, a bit of water, and bring to a boil, under cover. Add shrimp and simmer for 20 minutes. If served hot, spoon the sauce over the shrimp; if served cold, sprinkle with olive oil and parsley.

4 servings.

Mussels in White Wine
Midhje në verë të bardhë

2 pounds shelled large mussels
1/2 cup finely grated onions
1/2 cup oil
6 garlic cloves, finely sliced
1 tablespoon flour
1 cup white wine
1 cup chopped peeled tomatoes
2 tablespoons chopped parsley
3 bay leaves
Salt
Pepper

Simmer mussels in 1 cup salted water for 5 minutes. Sauté onion in oil; add garlic, sauté for 2 minutes, add flour, sauté for another 3 minutes, then stir in wine, tomatoes, parsley, bay leaves, salt and pepper. Add mussels and cook for 10 minutes over low heat, stirring occasionally. Serve immediately.

4 servings.

PASTA and PIES
BRUMRAT

Macaroni and Feta Cheese in Milk
Pastiço me djathë

2 cups milk
1 pound macaroni/noodles/spaghetti
Salt
3 tablespoons butter
3 eggs
1 cup diced feta cheese
Bechamel sauce, see p. 56
1/4 cup grated cheddar cheese
1/4 cup toasted whole-wheat-bread crumbs

Heat milk to simmering in a stock pot, then add macaroni/noodles/spaghetti so slowly that simmering does not stop. Add 1 teaspoon salt, cover and simmer until tender, or about 15–20 minutes. Put in a baking pan brushed with melted butter, add 3 eggs, feta cheese and 3 tablespoons butter, and mix well.

Prepare bechamel sauce according to recipe, p. 56, and smother the mixture with it. Sprinkle with cheese and bread crumbs and bake at 350°F until yellow-brownish.

Serve hot.
4 servings.

Macaroni and Ground Veal in Milk
Pastiço me kimë

2 cups milk
1 pound maccaroni/noodles/spaghetti
Salt
2 tablespoons butter
1/2 cup chopped onion
1/4 cup oil
1/2 pound ground veal
1/4 cup tomato juice
Pepper
Ground nutmeg
Bechamel sauce, see p. 56
1/4 cup minced cheese

Heat milk to simmering in a stock pot, then add maccaroni/noodles/spaghetti so slowly that simmering does not stop. Add 1 teaspoon salt and simmer until tender or about 15–20 minutes, then put in a baking pan brushed with melted butter. Sauté onion in oil, add meat and sauté until tender. Stir in tomato juice, season with salt, pepper and nutmeg, cook for 5 minutes over low heat, then stir this mixture into the baking pan.

Prepare bechamel sauce and spoon it over the mixture. Sprinkle with minced cheese and bake at 350°F until a brownish crust is obtained.

Serve hot.

4 servings.

Rice and Liver
Pilaf me mëlçi

1/2 pound lamb/chicken liver
1/4 cup finely grated onion
1/2 cup butter
2 cups brown rice
1/2 cup tomato juice
Salt
Pepper
3 cups beef bouillon

Sauté liver and onion in butter, add rice and sauté for 5 minutes. Add tomato juice, season with salt and pepper, sauté for 3 minutes. Stir in bouillon and simmer under cover until all liquid cooks away.
Serve immediately.
4 servings.

PIES
BYREQET

Albanian pies are generally made from thin pastry leaves, which can be rolled at home or bought at a grocery store. Most of the pies prepared by Albanian cooks are not sweet; instead, pie fillings are almost always salted. Thus, a piece of such a pie may well serve as the main dish of a meal.

Spinach Pie
Byrek me spinaq

1 cup oil, preferably olive oil
1 1/2 packets (or about 30) pastry leaves (phyllo dough)
1 1/2 pounds spinach, chopped
Salt
1 cup diced feta cheese
1/2 cup chopped green onions
2 eggs

Brush the baking pan with some of the oil, and start laying pastry leaves, allowing the edges to get out of the baking pan for about one inch: lay two leaves, sprinkle or brush with oil, then lay two other leaves, and so on, until half of the leaves are laid.

Sprinkle spinach with salt, then mix well—by hand—with feta cheese, oil, onions, eggs and salt, and spread this mixture over the laid pastry leaves. Finish laying the other half of pastry leaves, turn the edges of the bottom leaves over the pie, sprinkle with oil and bake in a moderate oven at 350°F for about 45 minutes or until a golden brown crust is obtained. Serve hot, accompanied with buttermilk, or beaten yogurt, thinned down in cold water, or with chilled stewed prunes.

Serves 6.

Leek Pie
Byrek me presh

1 1/2 pounds leeks, chopped
6 tablespoons butter or margarine
1/4 pound ground meat
3 eggs
Salt
Pepper
1 1/2 packets (or about 30) pastry leaves (phyllo dough)
1/2 cup oil

Sauté leeks in butter, add ground meat and sauté, remove from heat and mix with eggs, salt and pepper. Use this mixture as filling for the pie, which is prepared with the phyllo leaves and oil, and baked as in the recipe above (*spinach pie*).
Serves 6.

Cottage Cheese Pie
Byrek me gjizë

1 1/2 cups salted cottage cheese
3 eggs
4 tablespoons chopped parsley
Salt
6 tablespoons melted butter or margarine
1 1/2 packets pastry leaves (phyllo dough)

Mix well cottage cheese, eggs, parsley and a bit salt, and use this mixture as filling for the pie. Use melted butter/margarine to brush the baking pan and to sprinkle pastry leaves. Prepare and bake the pie as in the recipe *spinach pie*, p. 117.
4 servings.

Small Cheese Pies
Byreçka me djathë

2 cups chopped feta cheese/salted cottage cheese
2 eggs
2 tablespoons chopped parsley
1 cup melted butter/margarine
Salt
Pepper
3 cups pastry flour

Mix well feta cheese/cottage cheese with eggs, parsley, 1/4 cup butter and a bit salt and pepper.

Make pie dough by mixing flour with 2 1/2 cups water and a bit salt. Set aside for about 30 minutes, cut in half and roll each half 1/16 inch thick. Cut into several 4-inch wide long pieces. Sprinkle with butter, spread 1 tablespoon cheese mixture over a triangular area near one of the ends of each long piece, cover mixture with the triangular end of the long piece, and keep on folding left and right until a triangular roll is obtained. Sauté in butter until golden brown. Serve immediately.

4 servings.

Small triangular pies may also be prepared with ready-made pastry leaves/phyllo dough, and baked in a moderate oven at 350°F for about 30 minutes.

Milk Pie
Byrek me qumësht

1 package pastry leaves (phyllo dough)
1/2 cup melted salted butter/margarine
2 cups milk
3 eggs
1 cup grated feta cheese

Grill all pastry leaves except four over the stove elements until crisp and yellowish. Be cautious of open flame. Brush bottom of baking pan with some melted butter, lay two ungrilled leaves and sprinkle with butter. Mix well milk, eggs, cheese and butter. Lay grilled leaves in turn, sprinkling each of them with this mixture, saving two ungrilled leaves to lay on top. Sprinkle with butter and bake in moderate oven at 350°F for about 45 minutes.
4 servings.

Custard Pie
Qumështor

1/4 cup cornstarch
5 cups 2% milk, divided
1 1/2 cup sugar
Vanilla
5 eggs, beaten
1/2 cup melted butter, divided
1 package pastry leaves (phyllo dough)

Put cornstarch in a bowl, add 1 cup milk and mix well, to obtain a thin cream. Bring remaining milk to a boil, add the cornstarch mixture and stir continuously, to prevent lumps from forming. Add sugar and vanilla, let simmer 1 minute, and remove from heat. Chill until warm, then stir in beaten eggs with 1/4 cup butter, mixing continuously.

Lay half of the pastry leaves on the bottom of a baking pan brushed with melted butter, sprinkling every two of them with butter, and spread milk mixture over them; lay the other half of pastry leaves on top, sprinkling with butter as above. Bake in moderate oven at 350°F for about 30 minutes, until golden brown. Serve hot or chilled.

This pie can also be prepared by laying all the leaves at the bottom and covering them with the milk mixture. In such a case the pie is called *lakuriq* (naked pie).

4 servings.

CORNMEAL PIES
LAKROR

Spinach Cornmeal Pie
Lakror me spinaq

3 cups cornmeal, divided
1/4 cup oil
2 pounds chopped spinach
1/4 cup salted cottage cheese
1/4 cup olive oil
Salt
Dill
4 tablespoons melted butter

Pour half the cornmeal into a flat baking pan greased with oil. Add salted water until a thick mixture is obtained, then spread evenly. Put spinach in boiling salted water for a few seconds, remove, drain well and mix with cottage cheese, olive oil, salt and dill to taste. Add and spread this filling, cover evenly with cornmeal, baste with milk, sprinkle with butter and bake in moderate oven at 350°F for 15 minutes. Brown top slightly under broiler. Serve hot.

4 servings.

This pie is more delicious if patience dock or sorrel is used instead of spinach. In this case add a bit of menthe to the cottage cheese mixture.

Milk and Eggs Cornmeal Pie
Fli

4 eggs
3 cups 1% milk
2 cups cornmeal
Salt
1/4 cup melted salted butter/margarine, divided
1 pound chopped spinach
1/2 cup salted cottage cheese

Beat eggs in a large bowl, add milk and cornmeal, season with salt and stir well, until a thin dough is obtained. Pour 1/4 of the dough into a large buttered baking pan and spread evenly into a layer about 1/8–inch thick. Bake at 350°F for 10 minutes, sprinkle with butter and bake again for 10 minutes.

Mix well spinach with cottage cheese, spread the mixture evenly in the baking pan, cover with the remaining dough, sprinkle generously with butter and bake for 30 minutes. Cut in rhombic serving pieces; serve hot.

4 servings.

Ground Meat Cornmeal Pie
Lakror me kimá

1/2 cup finely grated onion
4 tablespoons oil
1 cup ground meat
1 cup milk
1/2 cup tomato juice
2 bay leaves
Salt
Pepper
2 cups cornmeal
3 eggs (keep 2 yolks separate)
2 tablespoons melted butter

Sauté onion slightly in oil, add meat and sauté for 5 minutes. Add 3 cups hot water and cook for 15 minutes, stirring constantly. Add milk, tomato juice, bay leaves, season with salt and pepper, and bring to a boil. Add cornmeal and stir constantly, to prevent lumping, until mixture thickens. Remove from heat and stir in eggs, saving two yolks. Pour the mixture into a flat oiled baking dish, and spread evenly. Beat two yolks in a bit of milk, season with salt and pepper, and smother the pie with it. Sprinkle with butter and bake in moderate oven at 350°F for 20 minutes. Cut in rhombic serving pieces. Serve hot.

4 servings.

Milk Cornmeal Pie
Oshmar

1/2 cup chopped feta cheese
1/4 cup melted salted butter/margarine/lard
3 cups 1% milk
2 cups cornmeal

Lightly sauté cheese in butter, add hot milk and bring to a boil. Add cornmeal, and stir constantly until mixture thickens and can be detached from the recipient. Pour into a large deep dish, let cool and cut in serving pieces. Serve hot.
4 servings.

SAUCES
SALCAT

You can easily make tasteful sauces in a few minutes, just by consulting any cookbook at hand. Hundreds of good recipes exist for cream sauces, herb sauces, tomato sauces, egg-and-butter sauces and so on, most of them bearing exotic names that cooks like to mention proudly to their guests. To make things easy we are giving here just a few recipes for sauces that are typically Albanian and have gained much popularity in Albanian cooking—delicious sauces, which will make your friends not only enjoy the food but also think you are an excellent cook.

Here are the recipes for three basic sauces, which can also serve as a base for other sauces: *brown sauce, white sauce cream sauce,* and *tomato juice sauce.*

Brown Sauce
Salcë e errët

1 teaspoon finely grated onion
1 tablespoon finely grated carrots
2 tablespoons butter/margarine
2 tablespoons flour
1 teaspoon finely grated garlic
1 cup tomato juice, or 2 tablespoons tomato sauce
2 cups soup stock, or meat broth
1/2 cup white wine
Salt
Pepper

Sauté onion and carrots slightly in butter, add flour, sauté for 1 minute, stir in garlic, sauté for 2 minutes, then add tomato juice (or tomato sauce diluted in a bit water), meat stock and wine. Season with salt and pepper and simmer for 45 minutes. If a clear brown sauce is preferred, you can pass it through a colander and simmer for another couple of minutes.

Yields 3 cups sauce.

Basic White Sauce
Salcë e bardhë bazë

2 tablespoons flour
3 tablespoons butter
2 cups meat/chicken broth
Salt
Pepper

Sauté flour slightly in butter, add meat broth stirring rapidly and constantly to avoid lumping, season with salt and pepper, remove from heat and drain. Serve with boiled meats or vegetables, or use as a base for other sauces.

Yields 2 cups sauce.

Cream Sauce
Salcë krem

4 tablespoons butter/margarine
3 tablespoons pastry flour
2 cups fresh milk, divided
1 teaspoon salt
1/4 teaspoon paprika
1/2 cup powdered milk

Melt butter/margarine in a saucepan; add and mix flour thoroughly without browning. Add 1 cup fresh milk gradually, stirring rapidly, until well blended. Add salt and paprika, simmer 10 minutes, then stir in a smooth mixture of 1 cup fresh milk and the powdered milk. Simmer 4 minutes, being careful that sauce does not boil.
Yields 2 cups sauce.

Tomato Juice Sauce
Salcë domate bazë

1/4 cup finely grated onion
1/2 cup chopped carrots
1 celery stalk, chopped
1/4 cup butter/margarine
1 tablespoon flour
2 cups meat broth
1 cup tomato juice
2 bay leaves
1 tablespoon chopped parsley
1 teaspoon finely grated garlic
Salt
Pepper

Sauté slightly onion, carrot and celery in butter; add flour and sauté until yellow. Add meat broth, tomato juice, bay leaves, parsley, garlic, salt and pepper, and simmer for 1 hour, stirring occasionally. Pass through colander and bring to a boil.
Serve hot, with broiled/fried meat, rice, noodles or other hot dishes.
Yields 3 cups sauce.

White Sauce with Onions
Salcë e bardhë me qepë

2 tablespoons flour
3 tablespoons butter/margarine
2 cups meat broth
1 cup finely grated onion
1 teaspoon finely grated carrots
1 tablespoon chopped parsley
Salt
Pepper

Sauté flour in butter over low heat until yellowish, add meat broth stirring constantly until a consistent mass is obtained. Add onion, carrot, parsley, salt and pepper, and simmer for 30 minutes. Pass through a colander. Serve with boiled meat, fish, seafood, cauliflower, etc.
Yields 2 cups sauce.

Tomato-Cream Sauce
Salcë domate-qumësht

1 tablespoon flour
2 tablespoons butter
1 cup meat broth
2 cups tomato juice
3/4 cup milk
Salt
Pepper

Sauté flour in butter until yellow, add meat broth and tomato juice, stirring constantly. Cook over low heat until sauce thick-ens, stir in milk and simmer for 2 minutes. Season with salt and pepper to taste. Serve hot, with fried meat, fish or seafood, or rice, noodles, etc.
Yields 3 cups sauce.

White Wine Sauce
Salcë me verë të bardhë

1/4 cup chopped onion
1/4 cup chopped celery
1 tablespoon flour
3 tablespoons butter, divided
1 cup white wine
2 cups basic white sauce (see recipe p. 126)
1 cup meat broth
Salt
Pepper
2 tablespoons lemon juice
1 tablespoon chopped parsley

Sauté onion, celery and flour in 2 tablespoons butter, stir in wine, add white sauce and meat broth, and cook over low heat for 20 minutes. Pass through a colander pressing with a spoon, and simmer for another 5 minutes. Season with salt, pepper, lemon juice, 1 tablespoon butter and remove from heat. Sprinkle with parsley. Serve with boiled meat or chicken, after simmering the meat in this sauce.
Yields 4 cups sauce.

Egg Cream Sauce
Salcë me vezë

1 cup cream sauce (see p. 126)
2 egg yolks
1/4 cup butter
2 tablespoons lemon juice

Just before serving heat the cream sauce and beat in egg yolks, butter and lemon juice. Serve with greens, fish, hard-cooked eggs, etc.
Yields 1 cup sauce.

Mayonnaise
Salcë majonezë

2 egg yolks
3 tablespoons lemon juice
1 teaspoon vinegar
1 teaspoon salt
1 1/2 cups olive oil

Combine and beat together egg yolks, lemon juice, vinegar and salt in a porcelain or earthenware bowl, being careful that beating is done in one direction only. Add 1 teaspoon oil slowly, beating constantly, until mixture thickens, add a second teaspoon oil, and keep on beating until all the oil is mixed. Keep in a cool place. Serve with fish, seafood, meat, salads, etc.
Yields 2 cups mayonnaise.

Spinach Mayonnaise
Majonezë me spinaq

1 cup finely chopped spinach
1/2 cup finely chopped parsley
2 cups mayonnaise
Salt
Pepper

Simmer spinach and parsley in a pot for 5 minutes. Drain, squeeze, mash, and pass through colander pressing with a spoon. Mix well with mayonnaise and season with salt and pepper. Serve with cold fish, ground meat rolls, etc.
Makes 2 cups.

Sardine Sauce
Salcë sardele

1 can sardines
1 cup mashed potatoes
1/4 cup grated cucumber pickles
2 tablespoons chopped parsley
1 tablespoon finely grated garlic
Salt
Pepper
1/4 cup olive oil
1/4 cup lemon juice

Mix well and mash sardines, potatoes, pickles, parsley and garlic in a bowl; season with salt, pepper. Add small quantities of oil, stirring constantly with a wire whip, until all oil is sucked by the mixture. Add lemon juice and stir until a uniform sauce is obtained.
Serve with fish or cold meats, sprinkled with parsley.
Makes 2 cups sauce.

Mustard and Sardines Sauce
Salcë mustardë-sardele

2 cans sardines
1 tablespoon finely grated onion
1 teaspoon finely grated garlic
3 egg yolks
1 tablespoon mustard powder
Salt
1/2 cup olive oil
2 tablespoons vinegar

Mash sardines, onion and garlic; add egg yolks, mustard and salt, mix well, then add oil and vinegar little by little until a uniform sauce is obtained. Serve with cold fish, meat etc.
Makes 2 cups sauce.

Mashed Potatoes Sauce
Salcë skordhan

1 pound mashed potatoes
6 garlic cloves, crushed
1/2 cup olive oil
1/4 cup vinegar
1/4 cup yogurt
Salt
Pepper

Mix well potatoes and garlic, then add oil and vinegar alternately and in small quantities, stirring constantly. Stir in yogurt and season with salt and pepper. Serve with fish or seafood, sugar beet salad etc.
Makes 3 cups sauce.

Pan Drippings Sauce
Salcë të pjekurash

Use pan drippings to prepare this easily made sauce: remove baked/broiled meat from the baking pan, simmer drippings until most of the water cooks away, sauté 1 tablespoon flour slightly, add 1 cup hot water stirring constantly, season with salt and pepper and simmer for 10 minutes. Serve hot, with baked or broiled meat.

PICKLES
TURSHITË

There is no such a thing as sweet pickles in Albanian cuisine. Oversweet pickles of vegetables or fruits are simply called jams or stewed fruits. The presence of vinegar in such jams or compotes just makes them unacceptable to people. A small amount of sugar may be present in some pickles, in which case they are not called pickles anymore, but *marinated vegetables*. As for fruit pickles, this term simply does not exist in Albanian. Fruits can only be cooked into stewed fruits, jam, jelly, or marmelade. By the way, there is a clear-cut distinction between fruits and vegetables in the Albanian language. Tomato, for instance, is never considered a fruit—just another vegetable. In order to be called a fruit, the product must be rich in sugars; otherwise it falls in the category of vegetables, and is good for salads, pickles, sauces, or for various hot dishes.

To prevent vitamins and minerals from being drawn out and discarded, which happens when vegetables are soaked in brine, you can add a small amount of calcium chloride to the pickling liquid. This salt is used to produce the delightful crispness of pickles, and may be purchased at a drugstore. It is absolutely harmless and at the same time it adds to the nutritive value of the pickles.

Pickled Sweet Peppers
Speca turshi

Celery leaves
Dill leaves
10 pounds whole peppers
1 cup salt
5 quarts water
2 cups vinegar
1 teaspoon calcium chloride
1/2 cup olive oil

Lay celery or dill leaves on the bottom of a large jar, and put a few layers of peppers as closely as possible on top. Put a weight over them—a heavy dish, for instance—lay celery or dill leaves, a few layers of peppers on top, and so on, until all peppers are laid, ending with a weight on top.

Stir in salt in hot water in a metal pot, bring to a boil and set aside for 12 hours. Add vinegar and pour the calcium chloride over peppers. Cover with a gauze and put the jar in a cool place for about 4 weeks. Pack firmly into pint or quart jars, finish filling jars with brine, add a bit of olive oil on top, seal and store.

PICKLED TOMATOES
DOMATE TURSHI

Choose green or yellowish (unripe) tomatoes and use the above recipe to prepare pickled tomatoes. When ready, pack firmly into jars, finish filling jars with brine, add a bit olive oil on top, seal and store.

Marinated Tomatoes
Domate marinadë

2 cups vinegar
1 cup water
1/4 cup olive oil
2 tablespoons salt + 1/4 teaspoon calcium chloride
1 tablespoon sugar
4 bay leaves
Pepper
Cinnamon
Clove
5 pounds green or yellowish tomatoes

Mix all the ingredients together except tomatoes, and bring to a boil. Wash tomatoes, put them in a large jar under weight, and pour the liquid over them. Cover the vase with a gauze and put in a cool place. After 3 days remove the liquid, bring to a boil, chill and return to the jar. Pack firmly into small jars, finish filling jars with marinade liquid, add a bit olive oil on top, seal and store.

You can follow the same procedure to prepare marinated cucumbers. Cucumbers are first soaked into boiling water and rinsed immediately with cold water. In addition to the above ingredients, you can add oregano, dill and a few garlic cloves.

Pickled Cucumbers
Tranguj turshi

10 pounds small cucumbers
2 cups vinegar
5 pints water
1 cup salt + 1 teaspoon calcium chloride
Dill
Celery

Prepare the mixture as in the above recipes and let cool. Lay celery leaves on the bottom of a large jar, and lay washed cucumbers vertically, firmly packed. Lay celery leaves between every two cucumber layers, put a wooden cover and a weight on top, pour mixture until cucumbers are completely dipped and there are still 5–6 inches left empty. Cover with a gauze and put in a cool place. In 4–5 weeks pickles are ready.

You can also put a few garlic cloves and oregano into the jar.

Pickled Cabbage
Lakër turshi

2 cups salt + 1 teaspoon calcium chloride
10 pints water
10 pounds head cabbage
2 cups vinegar
Celery
Dill

Stir salt and calcium chloride in water and bring to a boil. Let cool for 12 hours. Remove stems and green leaves from the cabbage heads and cut heads in half. Lay green cabbage leaves on the bottom of a large jar or of a wooden keg, put cabbage heads on top, and spread celery and dill leaves over them. Cover with an wooden lid or a heavy large dish, put a weight on top, then pour liquid and vinegar. Cabbage heads must be about 4 inches deep into the liquid. Cover jar/keg with a gauze and put in a cool place. Every 2–3 days remove the white layer that is formed on the surface, and after 2 weeks remove the liquid every 2 days, filter it and return to the jar/keg. In 3 weeks pickles are ready.

Cabbage Relish
Lakër turshi e grirë

10 pounds chopped cabbage
1 pound chopped beets
1 pound chopped green peppers
1/2 pound chopped carrots
8 cups water
1 cup vinegar
1 1/2 cup salt + 1 teaspoon calcium chloride
Celery stalk
Dill

Follow the same procedure as for cabbage pickles above. The relish will be ready in about 2 weeks.

Beet Relish
Panxhar i kuq turshi

6 pounds beets
1/2 cup vinegar
1/2 cup salt

Remove stems and simmer beets in 4 cups water until tender. Remove beets from liquid, rinse with cold water, peel, cut into halves, slice and put in a large jar together with the liquid. Prepare brine with the rest of the water, let cool, add vinegar and pour over beet. Relish is ready in 24 hours. Pack into small jars and finish filling with liquid.

Serve with peeled and sliced oranges and a bit olive oil.

Pickled Eggplant
Patëllxhanë turshi

2 pounds green peppers, diced
1 cup finely diced carrots
1 cup garlic cloves
12 tablespoons chopped parsley
4 tablespoons chopped celery
1 1/2 cups salt (divided) + 2 teaspoons calcium chloride
10 pounds small Italian eggplant
1/2 pound vine leaves
1 cup vinegar

Mix well peppers, carrots, garlic cloves, parsley, celery and 1/4 cup salt and use this mixture later as a filling for the eggplant.

Remove stems from eggplant, make a lengthwise cut and put them in a large pot with 1 gallon cold water and 1/4 cup salt for half an hour. Add 1 cup salt and 2 teaspoons calcium chloride to the cold water, bring to a boil, add eggplant and boil for a few minutes, until tender but not too tender. Drain and put in a large pan. Put a wooden lid and a weight over eggplant and leave aside for 12 hours to drain completely.

Lay vine leaves on the bottom of a large jar or keg, lay eggplant, pour vinegar, cover with vine leaves, put a weight on top and cover the jar/keg with a gauze. Put in a cool place and leave for 3 weeks to ferment.

COMPOTES and DESSERTS
KOMPOSTOT DHE ËMBËLSIRAT

FRUIT COMPOTES
KOMPOSTOT

In Albanian cooking compotes or stewed fruits are very popular. Generally they are not a combination of several fresh or canned fruits, but fresh fruits of one kind cooked in their own juice and sweetened generously. They are served cold, right from the refrigerator. Following are some suggestions for compotes:

Stewed Peaches
Komposto pjeshke

2 pounds peaches
1/2 teaspoon tartaric acid, or 1 tablespoon lemon juice
1 cup sugar
1 to 2 tablespoons liqueur wine

Peel and put peaches in 6 cups boiling water mixed with 1/2 teaspoon tartaric acid for 3 minutes. Drain, cut in halves, remove seeds and return seeds to the water. Stir in sugar and boil for 10 minutes.

Remove seeds, return peaches to the syrup, and bring to a boil. Chill, add liqueur wine and put into the refrigerator, or pack into jars, finish filling with syrup and seal. Serve cold, straight from the refrigerator.

Quince Compote
Komposto ftoi

2 pounds quinces
1 lemon (for juice and rind)
1 1/2 cups sugar
3 tablespoons liqueur wine

Wash quickly, dry and core quinces; cut each of them in about 16 slices, and put into 10 cups boiling water with lemon juice. Add sugar and simmer for 30 minutes, or until tender. Chill and add 1 teaspoon ground lemon rind and liqueur. Serve cold.

Prunes Compote
Komposto kumbulle

2 pounds prunes
2 quarts water
1 cup sugar
1 lemon (juice and rind)
1/4 cup liqueur wine

Wash quickly, dry, cut prunes in halves and remove stones. Bring water to the boil, add sugar and lemon juice, put in prunes and simmer for 2 minutes. Remove from heat, chill and stir in wine. Serve cold.

Follow the same procedure for appricots or nectarines.

Orange Compote
Komposto portokalli

2 pounds oranges
1 cup sugar

Grate rind of oranges, peel and slice, and put slices into serving cups until half full. Bring 6 cups water to a boil, add sugar and grated rind, and simmer for 8 minutes. Chill and pour over orange slices. Chill and serve.

Pears Compote
Komposto dardhe

2 pounds pears
3 tablespoons lemon juice
1 cup sugar
1 tablespoon grated lemon rind
1/4 cup liqueur wine
Cloves (whole)

Put peeled sliced pears with cores removed into 2 cups cold water and lemon juice for 20 minutes. Simmer pear peels for 10 minutes in 4 cups water in another utensil, filter the liquid, add sugar and return the syrup to the sliced pears. Chill and stir in wine. Season with cloves.

Cherry Compote
Komposto qershie

2 pounds cherries
1 cup sugar
1/4 cup liqueur wine
Cinnamon
2 tablespoons lemon juice

Remove stems, wash, dry and remove pits from cherries. Simmer pits for 8 minutes in 6 cups water, remove them and filter the liquid. Add sugar and cherries to the liquid, bring to a boil, and simmer for 1 minute. Chill and stir in wine, a bit cinnamon and lemon juice. Serve cold.
4 servings.

Apple Purée
Paluze mollësh

1 pound apples
4 cups water
3/4 cup sugar
2 tablespoons lemon juice
1 tablespoon starch
Cinnamon

Peel, remove the core and slice apples. Put into boiling water, simmer for 10 minutes, drain and squeeze through a colander. Return this purée to the liquid, add sugar and lemon juice, and bring to a boil. Stir in starch mixed with water and let boil for 1 minute. Pour into cups, sprinkle with cinnamon and chill. Serve cold.
Makes 4 servings.

DESSERTS
ËMBËLSIRAT

Stewed Dried Figs
Hoshaf me fiq të thatë

1 cup sugar
4 cups milk
1 cup finely grated dried figs
Cinnamon

Stir sugar in milk, bring to a boil and remove from heat. Add figs slowly, stirring continuously. Pour into earthenware serving bowls and bake in moderate oven (350°F) for 10 minutes. Chill and sprinkle with cinnamon. Serve cold.
Makes 4 servings.

Whole Wheat Jelly
Ashure

1 cup white whole wheat
6 cups water
1/4 cup cornstarch
1 1/2 cups sugar
3/4 cup shredded nuts
Cinnamon

Wash wheat and cook under pressure with water for 30 minutes, so that grains crack. Dissolve cornstarch in a little water, add wheat and liquid, add sugar and bring to a boil. Reduce heat to simmering, cook for 2 minutes, remove from heat and pour into serving bowls. Sprinkle with shredded nuts and cinnamon. Serve hot or cold.
6 servings.

Rice and Milk Cream
Sultiash

1/2 cup rice
4 cups milk
2 cups sugar
2 tablespoons cornstarch
Cinnamon

Put rice in a little water for 30 minutes, add boiling milk, and simmer for 30 minutes, stirring continuously. Add sugar and stir. Dissolve cornstarch in a little water and stir in slowly. Bring to a boil, remove from heat and pour into serving bowls. Chill and sprinkle with cinnamon.
4 servings.

Rice and Raisins
Kabuni

1 cup rice
1/4 cup butter
1 cup sugar, divided
1 1/2 cups mutton or lamb bouillon
1/4 cup raisins
Cinnamon
Ground cloves

Sauté rice slightly in butter mixed with a teaspoon sugar. Add boiling bouillon and raisins. Simmer 10 minutes, mix with sugar and bake in moderate oven (350°F) for 20 minutes. Remove from oven, sprinkle with cinnamon and cloves. Serve hot.
4 servings.

Halva
Hallvë

2 cups flour
1/2 pound butter
2 1/2 cups boiling water
1 cup sugar
1/2 cup shredded walnuts or almonds
Cinnamon

Sauté flour in butter in a saucepan until brownish, over medium heat, stirring continuously. Stir in boiling water and mix well, until all moisture cooks away. Add sugar and walnuts or almonds, and stir continuously, until a thick mixture is obtained that doesn't stick to the saucepan. Remove from heat, spoon halva into small dishes, and sprinkle with cinnamon. Serve hot or cold.
6 servings.

Cornstarch Halva
Hasude

1 1/2 cups sugar
2 1/2 cups water
3/4 cup butter
2 cups cornstarch

To prepare syrup: stir in sugar in water in a pot, bring to a boil, and cook over high heat until syrup spins a long thread. Melt butter in a saucepan and sauté starch until yellowish. Add 1 tablespoon sugar and mix well. Add syrup, stirring continuosly with a wooden spoon until a thick mixture is obtained that doesn't stick to the saucepan. Spoon halva in small dishes and serve hot or cold.
6 servings.

Cookies in Syrup
Sheqerpare

2 cups sugar, divided
Vanilla
Cloves (whole)
3/4 cup butter
2 egg yolks
2 cups all-purpose flour
1/4 teaspoon baking soda

To prepare syrup: put 1 cup sugar in 3/4 cup water, bring to a boil and cook until syrup spins a long thread. Remove from heat and season with vanilla and cloves.

Mix well remaining sugar and butter, add yolks and stir continuously. Add flour and baking soda, and stir into a soft dough. Lay dough flat on a large baking pan and cut into round pieces. Bake in moderate oven at 350°F for 30 minutes, let cool and stir in warm syrup. Serve cold.

Makes 6 servings.

Honey Cookies in Syrup
Shandatlie

2 1/2 cups sugar, divided
Vanilla
3 eggs, divided
4 tablespoons butter, divided
3 tablespoons honey
1/2 cup shredded walnuts
2 cups all-purpose flour
1/4 teaspoon baking soda

To prepare syrup: Stir 2 cups sugar in 1 1/2 cups water, bring to a boil and cook until syrup spins a long thread. Remove from heat, season with vanilla and leave aside.

Mix well 2 eggs, 1/2 cup sugar, 3 tablespoons butter, honey and walnuts, then add flour and baking soda and stir, but not too much. Pour dough into a baking dish brushed with butter, make it flat, brush the top with beaten egg, scratch the surface with a fork and bake in moderate oven at 350°F for 30 minutes. Remove from oven, chill and cut in rhomboid serving pieces about 2 1/2 inches wide. Pour warm syrup over and allow 2 hours for the cake to soak up syrup. Serve cold.

6 servings.

Baglava
Bakllava

3 cups granulated sugar
2 cups hot water
Ground cloves
7 1/2 cups flour
6 eggs, separated
1/2 teaspoon salt
2 cups cornstarch
3 cups shredded walnuts
1 cup cube sugar
2 cups melted butter

To prepare syrup: combine granulated sugar and water and cook over high heat until syrup spins a long thread. Season with ground cloves and leave aside.

Put flour into a large bowl, make a hole in the middle, add 5 yolks, one whole egg and salt, mix well and stir in enough water to make a dough. Knead dough until smooth, cover with a napkin and let it rest for 20 minutes. Make dough into small balls about 1 1/2 inches in diameter and leave aside on a board or large dish sprinkled with cornstarch. Roll each ball on a lightly starched board into a round sheet about 20 inches in diameter and as thin as paper. Spread these sheets over a large table covered with a clean napkin, let dry a little, then lay half of them on a round baking dish 20 inches in diameter, sprinkling every 2 pastry sheets with melted butter.
Pound walnuts with cube sugar in a mortar, a little at a time if mortar is not large enough. Lay this mixture over the laid pastry sheets, then lay the other half of sheets on top, sprinkling with melted butter as above. Cut baglava into rhombic serving pieces about 2 inches wide and bake in a preheated oven at 380°F for about 30 minutes, or until top of it becomes a brownish yellow. Remove from oven, cool, then pour the hot syrup over it. Serve cold.
12 servings.

REFRESHING DRINKS
PIJE FRESKUESE

Of various refreshing drinks served in Albania we will recommend just two: *bozë* and *hardiç*; both are fermented lightly sweetened drinks, delicious, healthy and really refreshing.

Millet Soft Drink
Bozë meli

7 1/2 cups millet flour
2 gallons water
1 package baker's yeast
5 cups sugar

Combine millet flour and water in a large jar, stir in baker's yeast, cover with a gauze and store in a cool place. Allow 3 days to ferment. Stir in sugar and store in the refrigerator. Serve cold.
12 servings.

Juniper Berries Wine
Hardiç

3 pounds juniper berries
3 gallons water
3 cups sugar

Wash and put berries in a wine cask with water, and allow 5 to 6 weeks to ferment, with the gas discharge hose plunged into a jar full of water. Stir in sugar and store in a dark cool place. Take out 1 to 2 quarts of wine every 2–3 days, and replace this amount with fresh water, but not more than 10 times. The wine tastes better if chilled first in the refrigerator before serving.

ENGLISH INDEX

153

ALBANIAN INDEX
INDEKSI SHQIP

Cookbooks from Hippocrene . . .

ALL ALONG THE DANUBE:

Marina Polvay

Recipes from Germany, Austria, Czechoslovakia, Yugoslavia, Hungary, Romania, and Bulgaria

For novices and gourmets, this unique cookbook offers a tempting variety of over 300 Central European recipes from the shores of the Danube River, bringing Old World flavor to today's dishes.

349 pages • 5½ x 8½ • numerous b/w photos & illustrations • 0-7818-0098-6 • W • $14.95pb • (491)

TASTE OF ROMANIA

Nicolae Klepper

"A brilliant cultural and culinary history . . . a collection of recipes to be treasured, tested and enjoyed."

—George Lang, owner of Café des Artistes

" . . . dishes like creamy cauliflower soup, sour cream-enriched mamaliga *(the Romanian polenta)*, lamb stewed in sauerkraut juice and scallions, and mititei *(exactly like the ones I tasted so long ago in Bucharest)* are simple and appealing . . . Klepper paints a pretty picture of his native country's culinary possibilities."

—Colman Andrews, *Saveur* magazine

A real taste of both Old World and modern Romanian culture. More than 140 recipes, including the specialty dishes of Romania's top chefs, are intermingled with fables, poetry, photos and illustrations in this comprehensive and well-organized guide to Romanian cuisine.

319 pages • 5½ x 8½ • photos/illustrations • 0-7818-0523-6 • W • $24.95hc • (637)

TRADITIONAL BULGARIAN COOKING

Atanas Slavov

This collection of over 125 authentic recipes, the first comprehensive Bulgarian cookbook published in English, spans the range of home cooking: including many stews and hearty soups using lamb or poultry and grilled meats, vegetables and cheese pastries; deserts of sweetmeats rich in sugar and honey, puddings, and dried fruit compotes.

200 pages • 5½ x 8½ • 0-7818-0581-3 • W • $22.50hc • (681)

THE BEST OF CZECH COOKING

Peter Trnka

Over 200 simple yet elegant recipes from this little-known cuisine.

248 pages • 5 x 8½ • 0-7818-0492-2 • W • $12.95pb • (376)

THE ART OF HUNGARIAN COOKING, Revised edition

Paul Pogany Bennett and Velma R. Clark

Whether you crave Chicken Paprika or Apple Strudel, these 222 authentic Hungarian recipes include a vast array of national favorites, from appetizers through desserts. Now updated with a concise guide to Hungarian wines!

225 pages • 5½ x 8½ • 18 b/w drawings • 0-7818-0586-4 • W • $11.95pb • (686)

ART OF LITHUANIAN COOKING

Maria Gieysztor de Gorgey

With over 150 recipes, this cookbook is a collection of traditional hearty Lithuanian favorites like Fresh Cucumber Soup, Lithuanian Meat Pockets, Hunter's Stew, Potato Zeppelins, and delicacies like Homemade Honey Liqueur and Easter Gypsy Cake.

236 pages • 5½ x 8½ • 0-7818-0610-0 • W • $22.50hc • (722)

THE ART OF TURKISH COOKING

Nesret Eren

"Her recipes are utterly mouthwatering, and I cannot remember a time when a book so inspired me to take pot in hand."
—Nika Hazelton, The New York Times Book Review

308 pages • 5½ x 8½ • 0-7818-0201-6 • W • $12.95pb • (162)

BEST OF GREEK CUISINE: COOKING WITH GEORGIA

Georgia Sarianides

Chef Georgia Sarianides offers a health-conscious approach to authentic Greek cookery with over 100 tempting low-fat, low-calorie recipes. Also includes helpful sections on Greek wines, using herbs and spices, and general food preparation tips.

176 pages • 5½ x 8½ • b/w line drawings • 0-7818-0545-7 • W • $19.95hc • (634)

TASTE OF MALTA

Claudia M. Caruana

Includes over 100 Maltese favorites like timpana (macaroni baked with tomatoes and ground meat enclosed in pastry), ross fil-forn (rice baked in meat sauce), and aljotta (fish soup with potatoes and garlic.)

250 pages • 5½ x 8½ • 0-7818-0524-4 • W • $24.95hc • (636)